STENWICK DAYS

*Rudolph Firth bolted through the snow as if all hell
was behind him.*

Stenwick Days

Orcadian stories by
R. T. JOHNSTON
with illustrations by the author

1984
THE ORKNEY PRESS

First published by *The Orkney Herald* in 1952 under the title *The Stenwick Annual*

Published in this edition by The Orkney Press Ltd., Victoria Street,
Stromness, Orkney

© Text and illustrations R. T. Johnston, 1984

ISBN 0 907618 09 X

Printed by The Kirkwall Press, *The Orcadian* Office, Victoria Street,
Kirkwall, Orkney

Bound by James Gowans Ltd., Glasgow

Contents

To EVA and
ALICE,
SHARLYN and
CLAIRE,
with love

Introduction

One day in the early thirties I was at Kirkwall Auction Mart to report the bull sale, and was pushing through the crowd to climb to the seat behind the auctioneer which the Press usually occupied, when I felt myself thumped on the shoulder and hailed with: "Hey boy, stey here a meenit."

I turned and found myself confronted by an elderly West Mainland farmer, whose acquaintance I had made a few months previously at a kirk function in Sandwick. He dealt me another amiable buffet and demanded: "Hey boy, is id right whit a'm been hearin' — that id's thee whar writes the pieces aboot Chohn Clouston in the pipper?"

I admitted that it was so, and he replied: "I wur telt that sam', bit I didno believe id. Thoo're a ferrylouper, er thoo no?"

I admitted that this, too, was the case, and he wagged his head in apparent perplexity, and inquired: "Bit my mighty, boy, whit wey is a ferrylouper writin' in the Orkney wey o' spickan?"

I said I supposed it was because nobody else was doing it and that it was a pity to waste such opportunities for humour as the Orkney dialect seemed to me to present.

My farming friend nodded and said: "Chist so. Weel, hed gaun, boy, for thoo're daein' no bed even if thoo er a ferrylouper."

He then bustled off to get a seat, having in that brief encounter, although I don't suppose he ever knew it, established himself in my mind as the model for Godfrey Ritch of Mucklegutter, who became probably the most popular character in all the Stenwick gallery.

What I had told him, that I started writing in Orkney dialect because nobody else was doing it, was quite true. It did not occur to me until later how odd it was that, neither in *The Orkney Herald* nor in *The Orcadian*, despite the abundant literary talents of their contributors, was anybody prepared, it seemed, to write in the local dialect — which was just as well for me because, if anybody had been doing it, I should certainly not have tried to get in on the act.

I could not say, without reference to the *Orkney Herald* files, when exactly the Stenwick stories began. In any case they didn't begin as stories. Soon after I joined the *Herald* as a reporter in the late summer of 1931 I began a weekly column of bits and pieces in which one or two fictional characters were introduced who poked mild fun at local happenings. There was no dialect; that came later. In the course of my reporting duties I had to go to the country districts quite a lot and it was there that the dialect particularly attracted me, as it was a good deal broader than the urban version. I began to store up words and phrases and eventually I introduced an Orkney farmer into my column — Chohn Clouston of Quoydunt. It was a brief appearance, just a paragraph or so and a few lines of conversation, but Chohn Clouston took readers' fancy so well that his appearances were expanded and he acquired a wife, Chessie; employees, Mansie and Peedie Tam; and neighbours — the Budges of Snortquoy, the Hourstons of Whassigo and the Harcuses of Rumtodly. Rumtodly, I may say here, was originally written as Rumtoddy, but my handwriting caused it to come up as Rumtodly, and as that it remained.

To the best of my recollection it was not for some time after the Quoydunt sketches started to appear that the parish in which the characters lived was named Stenwick — pronounced as written, not "Stennick." One result of my having a whole parish at my disposal was that more and more characters were introduced and gradually the sketches lengthened, displacing everything else from my column.

The first two Stenwick stories, as opposed to sketches, appeared not in the *Orkney Herald* but in successive issues of *Peace's Orkney Almanac*. This, as the older generation of readers will recall, was a comprehensive yearbook published by the *Herald* until it was, unhappily, killed off by the war. Each Almanac contained a number of stories, poems and articles. "The Rival Ploomen" was one of the Stenwick stories to appear, and the other was "Mansie's Wedding," which concerned Mansie of Quoydunt's marriage to Bella Budge.

I was often asked whether I had anybody special in mind

when I made up the Stenwick characters. Well, as I have already said, Godfrey Ritch was certainly drawn from life, with whiskers added to make him not too readily identifiable. Chohn Clouston himself was a composite figure, created out of three or four originals, as were Chessie Clouston, Willie Budge, Enoch Craigie, Eustace Rosie and a few others. With such as Silas Hourston of Whassigo, Chenet Cutt, the sub-postmistress, Geordie Manson the blacksmith, Police Constable Timothy Cursiter and Gregory Scarth of Pleeps, I had real people in mind when I launched them on their fictional careers, but even at this distance of time the less said about that the better. On the other hand, Boadicea Skea, the burly widow who carried on a vain hunt for a second man, Vernon Isbister, the parish scapegrace, Humphrey Bews the poet, Henrietta Kirkness, the domineering daughter of Godfrey Ritch, and the disagreeable Cuthbert Harcus had no counterparts in reality, but were merely invented out of the blue to add variety to the stories.

With the advent of the war, the curtain was about to drop on Stenwick activities, but I did keep writing the stories until my call-up, and wartime, in addition to seeing the establishment of the Stenwick Home Guard, also brought to the parish the beautiful Veronica, who came to Quoydunt to work as a landgirl and broke hearts right and left before she ultimately settled for marriage to the stalwart Tristram Mainland.

Stenwick did not completely vanish from the *Orkney Herald* once I had become a member of the RAF, but its appearances were rare. For one thing I had little time for writing anything other than letters home; for another I always disliked having to write at length by hand, and deprived of a typewriter I seldom felt like getting down to the chore of using pen or pencil.

However, I did send back an occasional Stenwick story to Kirkwall — maybe three or four — laboriously handwritten scripts which caused considerable puzzlement to the censoring officers, one of whom ordered me up in front of him to demand whether I was attempting to send coded reports to the Press. He was incredulous when I explained that I was merely writing a fictitious story for my old paper. "You mean to say they talk like this in Orkney?" he asked.

With the ending of the war the Stenwick stories resumed

in the *Orkney Herald* and continued until the *Herald's* unhappy demise in the early sixties. After that a number of the stories appeared in *The Orcadian*, at the request of Gerry Meyer, the then editor. By now, however, I was working in Aberdeen and finding the time hard to get for outside writing, so the Stenwick tales came to an end, until revived by Radio Orkney in the late seventies, and now, in handsome print, by The Orkney Press.

R. T. Johnston

Music hath charms

Looking out from between the two large piles of biscuit tins which made her shop window a fore-ordained also-ran in the contest to find Orkney's best-dressed window, Mrs Janet Manson, postmistress of Stenwick, saw three figures coming down the road and recognised them as the trio of personalities who bulked largest in the parish gossip of the moment. They were Boris Corsie of Netherdung, Medusa Wishart of Mucklebruck, and Nathaniel Swanney of Drycuithe.

For six months now Boris and Nathaniel had been wooing Medusa ardently, and the question all Stenwick was asking was, "Whar will shae tak?" It was not, however, an easy question to answer, and even Medusa, the person best placed to answer it, could not do so. Medusa seemed totally unable to decide between the two, and the inability worried her, the more so as she was a girl who disliked prolonging a delicate situation indefinitely. The other night her father had drawn her aside and had told her, with a certain curtness, "For goad's seck, lass, mak' up thee mind whar's coortin' thee, for a'm seek o' seein' yin two fellas in here for supper night efter night, an' if thoo kinno pick wen a'll keek the both o' them oot."

At times, it seemed to Medusa, Boris Corsie seemed the more desirable suitor, but just as she was on the point of informing Nathaniel that his chances were nil and that he had better direct his attention to some other girl while the blood of youth still ran hot in his veins, some hitherto unnoticed facet of Nathaniel's personality would obtrude itself upon her and his stock would rise with a rush.

As they drew abreast of the Post Office Medusa said, "Wett for me a meenit, berns. A'm gaun in here."

"A'll come in wi' thee," said Boris Corsie.

"So will I," said Nathaniel Swanney, giving Boris a sharp, suspicious glance.

"There's neun o' the two o' thee comin' in wi' me," snapped Medusa, "for a'm wantin' tae spick tae Chenet Cutt aboot some private metters."

"Cheust as thoo like, lass," said Boris, "bit dinno be lang, for when thoo're oot o' me sight the sun stops shinin'."

"Dis id, Boris?" asked Medusa. "Dis thoo think so an' all, Nathaniel?"

"Weel, I kinno say a'm notteeced id," said Nathaniel Swanney, a literally-minded individual, "for the sun is no been oot for days."

Medusa frowned a little as she turned to enter the shop. Nathaniel was not a patch on Boris when it came to making complimentary remarks. On the other hand, Boris was, if anything, too free with his pretty speeches. At the last Harvest Home she had overheard him saying the same thing, merely substituting the stars for the sun, to Audrey Craigie.

She pushed open the door and entered the shop, to the jangling clamour of the little bell which announced the advent of a customer.

○ ○ ○ ○ ○ ○

Boris Corsie leaned against the gable of the shop, lit a cigarette, and directed a pointed look at his rival.

"There's no need tae thee tae wett, Swenney," he said. "A'll see Medusa home tae Mucklebruck."

"Hid's all right," replied Nathaniel. "I dinno mind wettin'. A'm gaun no wey ither."

Boris Corsie's eyebrows drew together a little.

"Noo luk here, boy," he said sharply, "if I wis Medusa I wid be cheust aboot fed up wi' thee hingin' aboot whar thoo're no wanted. No doot thoo'll be hard the ould sayin' — two's company, an' three's a crowd."

"Yaas, a'm hard id," said Nathaniel, "an' thir's noathing tae hinder thee tae go home."

Boris laughed scoffingly. "Some hopp o' me gaun home. Boy, is id no dawn't on thee yet that thoo hisno a chance o' winnin' Medusa. All thoo're daein' is mak' theesel a deshed nuisance. I kinno get aheid wi' me coortin' as lang as thoo're aroond. A'm sheur Medusa disno want thee."

"All shae his tae dae is say id then," said Nathaniel evenly. "An' a'm no hard her sayin' id yet."

"Likely shae disno want tae hurt thee feelins. Bit no doot shae thinks thoo shid hiv the sense tae see that thoo're no wanted. Desh I widno care if thoo made yeuse o' the time thoo're wi' iss, bit thoo niver oppen thee mooth herdly."

"I get deshed little chance o' oppenin' id," retorted Nathaniel, with some bitterness, "for thee mooth's niver shut. It's yap, yap, yap all the time wi' thee. Medusa's heid min be ferly ringin' wi'd a mony a time."

Boris threw his cigarette to the ground and stamped his foot on it angrily.

"Luk here, Swenney," he said bluntly, "er thoo asked her tae mairry thee yet?"

"Er thoo?" asked Nathaniel warily.

"Fower times."

"An' noathing daein?"

"Weel, no yet, bit id's cheust a metter o' time noo. I ken be the wey shae luks at me that shae'll say yaas in a peedie while."

"Whit wey dis shae luk at thee?"

"Hid's diffeecult tae explain. A saft, tender kind o' wey."

"I ken the kind o' wey thoo mean," said Nathaniel, "a'm seen her lukkin' at me the same wey."

"Thoo're spickin' oot o' the back o' thee neck," said Boris huffily, and the conversation lapsed.

o o o o o o

Meanwhile, in the Post Office, Medusa had been opening her heart to Mrs Manson.

"I cheust hid tae come in here a meenit, Chenet," she said, "tae git awey fae them. Hid's fine in a wey tae hiv two men wantin' tae mairry thee, bit id's aafil herd on the nerves in a time."

"Yaas," agreed the postmistress, who had never been in the happy position of having two suitors, or she would never have married the one she did, "id min be kindo ackward, right enough."

"I kin niver get awey fae them," sighed Medusa, "they're always watchin' wen anither, tae mak' sheur a'm no wi' wen when the ither's no there. If wen comes tae the hoose tae see me the ither's no fer ahint, an' if wen meets me on the road the ither's sheur tae turn up in a peedie meenit. I dinno ken whit tae deu."

Janet Manson made a slightly impatient gesture. She would have liked to tell Medusa that in her (Janet's) opinion, she (Medusa) was a freck o' dirt, but Medusa was a good customer at the shop and it would have been foolish to antagonise her.

"I ken whit I wid dae," she said. "Tell wen o' them that thoo'll mairry him, an' the ither will clear oot, if he his ony menners at all."

"Yaas, bit whit wen?" wailed Medusa.

"Weel, thoo'll hiv tae mak' up thee mind aboot hid. Thoo'll hiv tae decide wen wey or the ither, seuner or litter, for thoo kinno mairry the both o' them, that's wen thing certain."

"I wish I kent whar tae tak'," said Medusa. "Id wid be aafil tae tak' wen, an' then find it wur the wrong wen."

"I wance read a storry," said Mrs Manson, somewhat inconsequentially, "aboot a lass what wis in love wi' two men, an' shae didno ken whar tae tak', so she made them fight a duel, an' that solved her diffeeculty, for wen wis killed an' shae mairried the ither."

Medusa pursed her lips. "I dinno think I wid like that. I widno like tae hiv onybody's blid on me conscience. Onywey, I herdly think fighting duels is allooed nooadays."

The postmistress did not think so either, but it had been a romantic idea.

"Weel, my mighty, Medusa," she suggested, "if thoo kinno decide ony ither wey, cheust toss a penny, an' if id comes doon heids mairry Corsie an' if id comes doon tells mairry Swenney."

"That's aafil like gamblin'," demurred Medusa.

"Weel, whit's mairrage bit a gamble onywey?" asked Mrs' Manson cynically.

"I wur up last night till weel after twelve," said Medusa, "makkin' oot a list o' thir qualifeecations as a hussband." She took a sheet of paper from her handbag. "Wid thoo like tae hear whit I wrott doon?"

"Tell me," said the postmistress eagerly.

"Here id is. Boris Corsie—the best lookin', bit wi' bendy legs an' gaun a peedie bit bald at the back o' the heid. Geud company, geud at makkin' me laugh, a grand kisser, an' geud at payin' me compleements. No aafil weel aff, bit chenerous wi' his money. Gies me plenty presents an' sweeties, an' tak's me tae plenty o' dances. A geud footballer—"

"Whit his bein' a geud footballer got tae deu wi' bein' a geud hussband?" broke in Janet.

"No muckle, I suppose," admitted Medusa, "bit I cheust thowt I wid pit id doon."

"Go on."

"That's for the credit side, as thoo might say. Noo, on the debit side—he's a peedie bit ower fond o' home brew, he smocks a lot, an' he his a wanderin' eye for ither lasses at times. That's all I hiv doon aboot Boris. Noo for Nathaniel. No aafil weel-like, bit wi' a geud heid o' hair, an' all his own teeth. A grand hand wi' a ploo, an' a herd worker. Fock weel aff, bit carefil wi' his money."

"Carefil," echoed Mrs Manson. "Doonright mean, I wid say."

"No, I widno say he wis mean. He says this is uncertain times, an' he disno approve o' squanderin' money, except he's gaun tae git geud value for id. Disno smock. Disno drink. Geud prospects. On the debit side—peur company, herdly oppens his mooth when he's wi' me, an' no very romantic tae be on a soffa wi', wi' the lights oot, for he'll niver spick aboot love, bit cheust aboot the stit o' the crops, an' the price o' feedin' stuff. No muckle o' a kisser, the wey his mooth is aafil weet. That's all I hiv aboot Nathaniel. Whit dis thoo think?"

Janet stared at her. "My mercy, Medusa, I wid say thir's no compareeson. Boris Corsie is fer aheid o' Nathaniel Swenney."

Medusa seemed surprised. "Lockars, dis thoo think so? I wid say thir cheust aboot equal. I wish thir wis some test I could mak' them dae for me, cheust tae shaw hoo muckle they think o' me, an' I wid mairry the wen whar made the best chob o' id."

At this moment there entered the Post Office, Barnabas Sabiston, leader of the musical combine known as the Stenwick Hill Billies, a boisterous young man who is chiefly responsible for organising dances, concerts, and entertainments generally in Stenwick, and the deus ex machina of this story, though the probability is that if anyone called him a deus ex machina to his face he would respond with a considerable lack of cordiality.

"Ay, Medusa," Barnabas greeted the daughter of Mucklebruck with an affable nod, "I thowt thoo wir here, for I saa thee two boy freends ootside, glowerin' at wen anither like the very deevil. Noo, Mrs Manson, will thoo stick this bill up in thee window or on the coonter, the wey fock kin see id, for id'll be the grettest attraction o' the 'ear in Stenwick."

And so saying he unrolled a large sheet of paper, handprinted in gaudy colours, and held it up for the inspection of the two ladies.

"Enormous Attraction," the bill ran. "Grand Concert in the Parish Hall, on Friday, 16th October, by Barnabas Sabiston and his Stenwick Hill Billies. Full Variety Programme by leading West Mainland Artistes, including Check Turfus. During the Programme there will be a Grand Crooning Contest, open to All Amateur Crooners in Stenwick, for the Parish Crooning Championship. No Entry Fee. Handsome Prizes. Barnabas Sabiston invites All Comers to Have a Go. Doors open 7 p.m., commence 7.30. Admission 2s, children 1s. Roll Up in your Thousands."

"Boy boy," said Mrs Manson, much impressed, "id shid be a gret affair, Barnabas, an' espeecially this croonin' contest. Id'll be a right pant. Is id for men an' weemin?"

"No," said Barnabas, "hid's cheust for men."

"I doot," said the postmistress, "thoo'll no git mony entries. The men in Stenwick is aafil faird for makkin' gappuses o' thirsels, an' crooners is no thowt muckle o' here onywey."

"Oh if I git a couple tae enter, that's all I need," said Barnabas lightly. He turned to Medusa. "Why no git Boris an' Nathaniel tae enter? Id might help thee tae pick the wen thoo're gaun tae mairry." And with a wave of his hand he left the shop.

In Medusa's eyes appeared the expression of one who has seen a great light.

"Feth," she cried, "that's the test a'm been wantin' tae pit. That's cheust whit a'll deu. A'll mak' them enter for the croonin' contest, an' tell them a'll mairry the winner o'd."

"Maybe neun o' the two o' them will win id," objected Mrs Manson.

"If thir's cheust the two o' them in for id, wen o' them's bound tae win id," retorted Medusa impatiently.

"Bit thoo dinno ken thir'll cheust be the two o' them in id."

"Dinno tell me the Stenwick men's gaun in for onything as daft as a croonin' contest except thir forced tae. No, thir'll cheust be Boris an' Nathaniel in id."

"H'm," said the postmistress, "thir no in id yit."

"They'll be, though," said Medusa with a jut of her jaw, "for a'll tell them that if they'll no dae a simple thing like enter for a croonin' contest for me seck a'm feenished wi' them both. An' if wen goes an' the ither disno, a'll mairry the wen whar goes, an' as fer as a'm concerned the ither kin go an' chump in the Loch o' Stenwick."

"Weel, plaze theesel, Medusa," said Mrs Manson with a shrug. "Id's wen wey o' pickin' a man. Id widno be me wey. Whar wants a hussband whar kin croon?"

"Seein' that id's gaun tae be me hussband," snapped Medusa, "cheust thoo let me worry aboot that." She moved to the door, pausing to say, "An' by the wey, Chenet, thoo'll maybe be geud enough tae trit whit a'm said tae thee as confeedential. I dinno want me intention tae git aroond."

She had scarcely closed the door behind her when the parish bush telegraph, of which Mrs Manson is the nerve centre, crackled into action. Less than an hour later, all Stenwick knew of the vital issues that were to hang on the crooning contest.

○○○○○○

When Medusa joined her two suitors outside the Post Office they could tell instantly that something was brewing, by the sparkle in her eye, and the speculative glances she kept darting from one to the other. It was not, however, till they had escorted her to the gates of Mucklebruck that they were enlightened.

"Weel," she announced, "a'm made up me mind whar a'm gaun tae mairry."

There was what is popularly known as a pregnant silence.

Then Boris Corsie took a deep breath, and asked, "Whar?"

"The wen," said Medusa, "whar wins the croonin' contest.

"Whit croonin' contest?" asked Boris.

Medusa explained, and there was another pregnant silence. Boris chewed his underlip. As for Nathaniel, he shrank visibly.

"Thoo mean," said Nathaniel, in a hollow voice, "thoo want iss tae go up on the stage, an' sing in front o' fock?"

"That's right."

A tremor ran through Nathaniel. A shy, backward individual, mouthless even in the society of his closest friends, he found the thought of appearing in front of an audience, let alone singing to it, one that struck terror to his soul.

"In that case," he stated flatly, "thoo kin coont me oot."

Medusa's lips tightened.

"Thoo'll no deu id?"

"I couldno, no for love or money."

"No even for both? Thoo'll git me if thoo win, an' thir's a prize o' five pound as weel."

Nathaniel shook his head. Medusa turned to Boris. "Whit aboot thee?"

Boris is scarcely of so retiring a disposition as Nathaniel, and as a member of the Stenwick football team he is frequently in the public eye. Still, even he quailed at the prospect of appearing in a crooning contest. For him the footlights held no magic. Only once in his life had he appeared on the stage, and it had been an experience of which he had gruesome recollections. At the age of eight he had been cajoled into participating, at a Sunday School soiree, in an ensemble entitled "Who Killed Cock Robin?" His had not been the leading role, nor even a particularly exacting one. All he had been required to do was step forward, at a given cue, and intone the lines:

> "I, said the owl,
>   With my little trowel,
>   I'll dig the grave,"

yet, on the night of the performance he had made the most frightful botch of this simple task, and had fled in humiliation from the platform, pursued by the jeers and catcalls of the audience. Even yet the memory made his flesh creep.

"Weel, Medusa," he replied, "I kinno say I think muckle o' the idea. Kin thoo no think o' a better way o' decidin'?"

The girl's eyes flashed. "No. An' a'm no gaun tae try. If thoo'll fail hert on a peedie thing like this, thoo're no muckle worth."

Boris sighed. "Weel, a'll mak' an aafil gappus o' mesei, bit a'll dae id."

"Geud on thee, boy. That settles id than, for if thoo're gaun tae enter an' Nathaniel Swenney is no thir's no need—"

"Wett," broke in Nathaniel, in a strangled voice.

"Weel?" inquired Medusa eagerly.

The agonised contortions of Swanney's face were evidence of the struggle that was going on within him. His whole being recoiled from the prospect of singing on the stage as an Aberdeen-Angus breeder recoils from the sight of a herd of Friesians, but, shy as he is, there is a dour quality about Nathaniel Swanney that makes him resent giving in without a struggle. Ultimately he bowed his head, in the attitude of one accepting his fate, and muttered: "A'll enter for the contest teu."

"Weel spocken," cried Medusa. "Noo, thoo'll better both go right home an' start tae practeese."

○ ○ ○ ○ ○ ○

The arrival of Friday evening saw the Parish Hall packed to its doors. Barnabas Sabiston's concerts were always popular, but never had there been one as popular as this. It was a complete sell-out. Long before the curtain was due to rise people were standing round the sides of the hall and clinging to the window sills. The last time the Parish Hall had held such a throng had been when Persephone Garson, a bright young thing just demobbed from the Waafs, had been billed to do a fan dance, an intention which had unfortunately been nipped in the bud by the Kirk Session. The reason for the huge crowd was, of course, the appearance in the crooning contest of Boris and Nathaniel, for all Stenwick knew that the winner was to receive, in addition to the five pound prize, the hand of Medusa Wishart.

As Medusa herself had shrewdly foreseen, Boris and Nathaniel were the only competitors, so that it was clear that a decision would be reached in the marital stakes one way or the other.

Boris and Nathaniel were to do their stuff, Barnabas had told them, immediately prior to the interval. Till then they had merely to wait in the dressing-room and take it easy. They were now waiting, but finding it hard to take it easy. As item followed item, and zero hour approached, both were getting into a state of nervous tension that developed with increasing rapidity. They manifested this in accordance with their respective temperaments. Boris paced up and down the room, feverishly smoking cigarette after cigarette, biting his nails, and muttering incessantly the words of 'The Rose of Tralee', which he had elected to render. From time to time he darted to the crack in the wall which enabled a view to be had of the audience, and he was disturbed to observe, in the front, or ringside seats, a considerable number of his colleagues of the football team. During the past few days he had had to endure no little chaff from the football team on the subject of his crooning, good-natured, it was true, but he had sensed an undertone of resentment that one of their number should let the team down by stooping so low as enter for a crooning contest.

About the quality of his crooning Boris was under no delusions. He had been practising hard at Netherdung, but he had quickly realised that he must be an exception to the adage that practice makes perfection. It might be coincidence that since he had started practising, two of his father's employees had given notice, his sister's canary had died, and the collie had run away, but he did not think so. He could only hope that Nathaniel Swanney's crooning was worse than his own.

As for Nathaniel, he was sitting bolt upright in a chair in the corner of the room, his fingers outspread on his knees, his eyes fixed on the opposite wall in a ghastly, unseeing stare. But for the fact that now and again his tongue flicked from his mouth to lick his dry lips he might have been taken for a corpse.

Into the dressing-room came Barnabas Sabiston, beaming more expansively than usual, for he stood to line his pockets well off this evening's entertainment.

"Weel, boys," he said, "hoo er thoo feelin'? Hid'll no be lang noo. Check Turfus is cheust gaun on, an' thoo're efter him."

Boris Corsie gulped a little. "Could — could thoo no pit iss litter on in the programme, boy?" he pleaded.

Barnabas frowned. "Kinno be deun, boy. The audience widno like id. Whit's wrang wi' thee? Thoo're no faird o' gaun on, er thoo?"

"I am hid," muttered Boris.

"Thoo'll be all right wance thoo're oot on the stage," said Barnabas reassuringly. "Dae thee best noo, an' dinno let thee lass doon. Shae's a right nice lass, Medusa. A'm cheust been spickan tae her."

"Is shae here?"

"Of coorse shae's here. Shae kens geud singin' when shae hears id teu. Shae wur compleementin' me on me solo. Shae said shae hid niver hard 'The Rose o' Tralee' sung better."

Boris started. " 'The Rose o' Tralee.' Did thoo sing hid?"

"Yaas."

"That's whit a'm singin' in the contest."

"Desh that," said Barnabas in irritation. "Kin thoo no sing something ither?"

"I dinno ken noathing ither."

Barnabas shrugged. "Oh weel, id kinno be helped. A'll go noo. A'll gie thee a shout when id's time tae thee tae go on the stage." He cocked an ear appreciatively as, from the platform, there came the thunderous vibrations of Check Turfus's imitation of a bull bogling. "Check's in gret form the night. He'll sure tae get an encore, so that means thoo hiv aboot five meenits yet."

He moved over to Nathaniel Swanney, who had neither moved nor spoken during the conversation, and slapped him on the shoulder with a hearty, "Cheer up, boy." Nathaniel leaped to his feet with a ringing screech, as if a hornet had stung him, pivoted twice, and dropped back into his chair in the same attitude as before. Barnabas surveyed him thoughtfully. "Geud," he remarked, "he's no in a fit stit tae go an' croon. His thoo no a drem thoo kin gie him, boy?"

"He disno touch the stuff," explained Boris.

"Weel, weel," said Barnabas, and left the dressing-room, shrugging his shoulders. From outside came a deafening roar of applause, signifying that Check Turfus had just concluded his imitation of a bull bogling, but as Barnabas had foreseen there followed a clamour for an encore such as few artistes, and certainly not Check Turfus, could resist.

It occurred to Boris Corsie that Barnabas Sabiston's suggestion of a dram was a good one. He had a half bottle of whisky in his pocket, and though he had intended to croon without the aid of Dutch courage, the strain on his nerves had become such that flesh and blood could resist it no longer.

He took out the bottle, uncorked it, and helped himself to a generous swig, and was about to pocket the bottle again when he noticed Nathaniel Swanney staring at it yearningly. Boris's first thought was, "Desh him, whit wey shid I gie him ony help?" but in spite of himself he was touched by the stark misery on Swanney's face.

"Here, boy," he grunted, "tak' a sook at this. Thoo luk as if thoo need id." And he extended the bottle.

Swanney hesitated for a moment, as if reluctant to break his lifelong abstinence, then he snatched the bottle, and tilted it to his lips.

Boris watched tolerantly, expecting to see his rival break into a fit of choking after the first sip, but the bottle remained at Swanney's mouth, and rose slowly from the horizontal to the vertical.

"That'll deu, boy," cried Boris in alarm, "my mercy that'll—"

Nathaniel handed back the bottle, empty.

"My geud goad," gasped Boris, "thoo're feenished id."

Nathaniel drew his hand across his mouth, "Yin wur geud," he said.

He got to his feet, and stood there somewhat waveringly. There was a flush on his face, and a sparkle in his eye. He hiccupped violently. "I feel—hic—gret," he announced.

Barnabas Sabiston appeared in the doorway. "Come awey boys," he said. "Id's time for the contest." He noted with gratification the more animated demeanour of Swanney, drawing the obvious conclusion from the bottle in Boris's hand.

"I thowt thoo said he niver touched id," he commented.

"Touched id," grunted Boris. "He's feenished id."

"All the better," said Barnabas. "Noo, come awey."

o o o o o o

There was a deafening roar from the audience, not of applause, but of laughter, as Barnabas led Boris and Nathaniel on to the stage, for Nathaniel for some reason known only to himself, had turned his cap back to front, and had rolled up the legs of his trousers, displaying a pair of yellow socks held up by mauve and vermilion suspenders. The laughter intensified as Swanney, reaching the centre of the stage, began to cavort in small circles, in a grotesque semblance of a Highland Fling. Boris eyed this performance gloomily, thinking how ironic it was that it had been himself who had put Nathaniel into this carefree frame of mind. Already, without even having started to croon, Nathaniel was well on the way to being the hit of the show, while he, Boris Corsie, was twice as self-conscious as before.

"Ladies an' chentlemen," announced Barnabas, "wae noo come tae the highspot o' the evenin', a contest for the croonin' championship o' Stenwick. As thoo see, wae hiv two competeetors, both o' them weel known, Nathaniel Swenney o' Drycuithe—" here Nathaniel skipped forward, swept off his cap and bowed low with a wide and fatuous grin, "—an' Boris Corsie o' Netherdung." Boris looked sheepishly down at the platform, and shuffled his feet.

"This contest," proceeded Barnabas, "will be judged be the audience, the competeetor whar gits the loodest applause tae be the winner. The winner will receive a prize o' a five pound nott, an' thir'll be a conseelation prize o' ten bob for the ither competeetor. An' noo a'll call on the first competeetor, Boris Corsie, whar is gaun tae croon 'The Rose o' Tralee'."

There was a murmur from the audience at this, which was put into words by old Godfrey Ritch, who bawled from the fifth row, "Wur hard hid already."

"A'm pointed hid oot tae Boris," said Barnabas, "bit id seems id's the only wen he kens."

Boris stepped forward, while Barnabas, who was accompanying, sat down at the piano. There was a light sweat on Boris's face, and the massed faces of the audience seemed to swim before his eyes. He took a deep breath, and as the piano tinkled he burst into song.

The audience listened with increasing restlessness. Musical standards in Stenwick are by no means high, but when an audience has heard 'The Rose of Tralee' sung well, it is apt to be impatient of a second rendering by someone who sounds like a bullfrog suffering from laryngitis, which is a not inaccurate description of Boris Corsie's voice. Thus when Boris concluded the first verse there was a stony silence, broken by a remark from Jasper Jolly, one of the vocalist's football team-mates: "Boy, come doon fae there. Thoo're hoppless."

As Boris began the second verse the audience's hostility became less passive. Old Ritch bawled, "Stoop, for goad's seck," and several rolled-up programmes were flung at the stage, one of which hit Boris between the eyes. Boris sang on grimly, but with ebbing hopes. In the fourth row of the audience he saw Medusa, and on her face was an expression of intense repugnance. Rolled-up programmes began to shower around him. He floundered, halted, and stammered, "A'm forgot the rest o' the wirds."

"Thank the Pope for hid," yelled Jasper Jolly derisively, and Boris, head bowed, withdrew to the rear of the stage.

"An' noo," said Barnabas, "a'll call on wur second competeetor, whar is gaun tae croon—" He glanced questioningly towards Nathaniel, who retorted promptly, "Whit will we deu wi' the Dounby Lasses."

Nathaniel advanced with a rollicking swagger to the front of the stage, and without waiting for the piano, unbuttoned his jacket, stuck his thumbs in the armholes of his waistcoat, executed an impromptu little step dance, and launched into the well-known and slightly scandalous ditty.

"Whit will we deu wi' the Dounby Lasses" does not altogether lend itself to crooning, and Nathaniel did not attempt to croon it. He roared it out at the top of his voice, improvising lines to replace those which escaped his memory, prancing back and forth between verses like a high-spirited foal, kicking up his heels, waving his arms, and for variety accompanying himself on an imaginary accordion. Between the quality of Nathaniel's voice and Boris's there was little to choose. If Boris's resembled that of a bullfrog with laryngitis Nathaniel's was like that of a crow with croup, but in the technique of putting a number across there was no comparison. Nathaniel left Boris standing, and when he finished it was to an ovation that nearly ripped the rafters of the hall from their sockets.

"Weel, fock," said the grinning Barnabas Sabiston, "thir's no doot whar's the winner o' this contest. I hiv gret pleasure in declarin' Nathaniel Swenney the croonin' champion o' Stenwick, and in hendin' him the five pound nott first prize."

○ ○ ○ ○ ○ ○

It was a glum-faced Boris Corsie who, ten minutes later, wandered out of the dressing-room and round to the back of the hall, to smoke a cigarette and consider his defeat. His mind was seared with the knowledge that by giving Swanney that whisky he had compassed his own downfall, but who, he asked himself forlornly, could have foreseen that the

In the technique of putting a number across, Nathaniel Swanney left Boris Corsie standing.

gesture would transform a stolid tongue-tied clurt into a veritable Harry Lauder. He sighed. Ah well, life was like that, and it was perhaps better to have loved and lost than never to have loved at all.

Just then he found himself joined by Nathaniel Swanney, but a Nathaniel of considerably less exuberant demeanour than when Boris had last seen him.

"Weel?" grunted Boris, "I suppose thoo're comed tae glot ower me. Or er thoo gaun tae invite me tae the weddeen?"

"Thir'll be no weddeen," said Nathaniel shortly. "No as fer as a'm concerned onywey."

Boris stared at him.

"Whit dis thoo mean? Er thoo no gaun tae mairry Medusa?"

"Shae's no gaun tae mairry me. A'm cheust been spickan tae her. Shae said that efter yin exheebition shae couldno stend the thowt o' mairryin' ony o' the two o' iss."

"My giddy geud. The deshed bizzom indeed, brakkin' her promeese. So shae's gaun tae mairry nobody."

"Shae's gaun tae mairry Barnabas Sabeeston. She telt me shae hid come tae the conclusion that him an' her wis made for wen anither."

"So wae cheust made geups o' wirsels for noathing," said Boris. His lips tightened. "That's weemin for thee."

"That's weemin," agreed Nathaniel.

There was a short silence.

"When time dis the ber at Dounby shut?" asked Nathaniel presently. "I hiv a five pound nott I wid like tae spend."

"An' I hiv ten bob," said Boris. He glanced at his watch. "If wur queek wae kin hiv half an' oor there."

As they pedalled furiously up the road to Dounby Nathaniel remarked, in tones of satisfaction: "Thir's wen thing I hiv tae thank Medusa for. If id hidno been for her I widno ken whit a grand tist thir is wi' whisky."

Out of the past

It was an unusually benign day for autumn, and old Godfrey Ritch, as he leaned against his gate-post of his farm of Mucklegutter, felt his eighty-seven years resting lightly upon his shoulders. "Yaas," he said to himself, "id's a grand day," and it occurred to him that it would be a good idea to take a chair out to the roadside and sit there for an hour or so, with a jug of home brew at his elbow, viewing the passing scene.

There was actually not much to view, there being not a living thing in sight, except Mainland of Drydivot's Shorthorn bull, which was pacing thoughtfully on the skyline, bogling resonantly from time to time. However, Godfrey reflected, when one had a jug of home brew at one's elbow, there was no need to worry overmuch about the lack of animation in the landscape.

He was just about to turn towards the farmhouse and bawl for his daughter Henrietta to bring him a jug of home brew and a chair, in that order, when there appeared on the road the Post Office van, its red body glinting brilliantly in the afternoon sunlight. It approached Mucklegutter rapidly and drew to a stop at the gate. The driver, one Alaric Walls, poked his head out from the side window.

"Ay, Godfrey," he greeted the veteran, "thir's a couple o' letters for thee." He handed them forth, and with an affable "Cheerio" let in his clutch, and was off in a cloud of dust.

Godfrey inspected the letters. One was merely his weekly football pool coupon, sent by Messrs Littlewood; the other caused him to frown in some puzzlement. It was postmarked Aberdeen, and was addressed, in sprawling ill-written characters, to "G. Ritch, Stenwick, Orkney." To the best of his recollection Godfrey had never seen this handwriting before.

"I winder," he mused, "whar this kin be fae." Realising

that there was an obvious way of finding out he slit it open, and took out the single sheet of notepaper it contained. It was a short, and not particularly sweet letter. Ignoring the customary formality of "Dear Sir," it began: "Thoo ould swindler, if thoo're no deid when thoo get this thoo seun will be, for a'm on me wey tae tak' me revenge for whit thoo did tae me fether, forty year ago. Say thee prayers, for a'll be here near as seun as this letter." It was signed, "Noah Pottinger."

"Noah Pottinger," muttered Godfrey. "Whaur in the neem o' — ?" And then a lightning flash of recollection seared through his brain. "Geud goad, id's ould Rupert Pottinger's son." His ruddy face went ashen. His staff dropped from his nerveless hand. The sun was still shining brilliantly but it seemed to the veteran that the afternoon had suddenly gone dark. He glanced fearfully up and down the road, and gulped with relief to find that there was not a soul in sight. All thought of a chair by the roadside and a jug of home brew gone, he shambled hastily towards the farmhouse, where, once inside, he locked and bolted front door and back. Then he bawled for his daughter.

"Henrietta. Whar the dickens er thoo? Come here, for mercy's seck."

His daughter scurried downstairs fearing that her father had perhaps suffered one of his periodic heart attacks. She found him pacing the kitchen like an elderly panther.

"Whar's me shotgun?" he demanded.

Henrietta stared at him. "Thee shotgun, fether. Geud, hid'll be whar thoo pat id when the Home Guard wur disbended. Up in the attic."

"Git id, queek," shouted the veteran, "for a'll maybe need id ony meenit."

"Weel, weel," said Henrietta, "bit whit's all this aboot? Thoo're no gaun shootin' rebbits at thee time o' life sheurly?"

"Hid's something a piece bigger than a rebbit a'll be shootin' at," replied her father grimly. "Luk at this letter a'm cheust got."

He handed her the letter. Henrietta read it in some mystification.

"Whar's this Noah Pottinger, an' whit wur id thoo did tae his fether that's pitten him so wild?"

"He's a son o' ould Rupert Pottinger, whar wrowt for me a mony a 'ear ago. Thoo'll no mind him on, for I hidno still mairried me second wife, an' thoo wurno born."

"I wid think no, indeed," snapped Henrietta, "if thoo wurno still mairried tae me mither."

"Hed thee yap till I tell thee," snarled her father. "Wen day Rupert Pottinger cam' tae me, an' telt me he hid saved a hunder an' fifty pound, an' he wur gaun tae buy a peedie ferm—in fact, id wur the ferm o' Ratbister, whit Obadiah Corrigall his noo. Weel, he said he wur gaun in a month's time, an' he wanted me tae keep his money in the fermhoose for seff keepin' till he wur ready tae hend id ower. So I took the money an' pat id in the draar. Noo, this wur cheust aboot the time that the Derby wur being run, an' I hid gotten a tip fae a freend o' mine in the sooth tae say that thir wis wen horse in the riss whit wid be an aisy winner, an' tellin' me tae be sheur an' pit me sark on id."

"Whit a daft thing tae deu," said Henrietta. "Pit thee sark on a horse."

"Will thoo stoop? Id's cheust a wey o' spickan. Whit he meant wur that I shid back the aneemil as herd as I could, for id wur runnin' at 30 tae one, an' thir wis a fortune tae be made on id."

"Whit," inquired Henrietta, "is all this got tae deu wi' Rupert Pottinger?"

"Wett till I tell thee," snorted Godfrey. "Weel, I wur aafil herd up in them days, an I thowt whit a peety id wur that this chance o' makkin' a fortune wur gaun tae wist, the wey I hid noathing tae back the horse wi'. An' then —"

"Thoo thowt aboot Pottinger's hunder an' fifty pound in thee draar," cut in Henrietta, who knows the way her father's mind works when the gambling fever gets into his blood.

"Yaas," admitted Godfrey. "At first I thowt on askin' Rupert for a len' o' the money, an' then I thowt he widno be aafil keen on the idea, so I cheust took the money, an' pat id awey tae me freend in the sooth tae back the horse."

"Bit geud secks, fether, that wur stealin'."

Godfrey shuffled his feet awkwardly.

"That wurno the wey I lukked at id. The wey I saa id, the horse couldno loss, an' I wid mak' fower thoosand five hunder pound, an' I wid gie Rupert his money back, wi' a peedie bit extra for the yeuse o'd."

"Bit the horse lost."

"Yaas, id lost," and Godfrey's face contorted, for even after all these years it was a bitter recollection.

"An' Rupert Pottinger's money wur lost teu."

"Yaas."

"Whit did he say?"

"He wur fer fae plazed, a'll tell thee. He didno tak' id in a philosopheecal wey at all. In fact, he wur ferly barmin'. He chissed me roond the ferm wi' a scythe, an' then when he caamed doon a bit I telt him that id wur cheust the luck o' the game, an' that life wur full o' ups an' doons, an' that the next time wur luck might be in. I suggestit that he shid save some more money, an' I wid pit id on a better horse the next 'ear, bit he widno hear o' id."

"A'm no surprised," said Henrietta.

"Of coorse I said I wid pey him back, bit id widno be for a lang time, an' in the meantime he shid stey an' work for me as yeusual, bit he said he widno work for me if he wur stervin', an' the next day he gied tae a chob in Birsay, an' efter that he gied tae a chob in Sooth Ronaldshay. Noo an' again he wid write me an' ask when I wur gaun tae pey him back some o' his money, bit I hid no money tae spare, an' I hard he hid emeegretted tae Austrellia, an' wur gotten a chob there as a kengaroo."

"A kengaroo's an aneemil," said Henrietta.

"Is id, lass? Weel maybe id wur a chob lukkin' efter kengaroos, I dinno ken. Onywey his son's comin' efter me blid, so dinno stend there dortin' ony langer, bit go an' git me gun."

All the time he had been telling his tale Godfrey had been scurrying to the window for agitated glances up and down the road, but so far, to his relief, no-one had appeared in sight.

○ ○ ○ ○ ○ ○

Henrietta came down from the attic with the shotgun, and Godfrey surveyed it dubiously. It was dusty and rusty, and generally in poor condition, for it had not been used since the famous airborne invasion scare of 1941, when an Army transport plane had force-landed in a field near Mucklegutter, and Godfrey had let daylight through a couple of high-ranking British staff officers before it had been explained to him that he was not dealing with the enemy. However, five minutes with a piece of rag and a pullthrough, and it would no doubt be serviceable enough to blow the avenging Noah Pottinger into an assortment of pieces.

"Whar's the ammuneetion?" he demanded.

"Lockars fether, thir's no ammuneetion. Dis thoo no mind, thoo hended id all in when the war wis deun."

The veteran smote his forehead.

"My giddy geud, so I did. Whit a feul. Me gun's no deshed yeuse wantin' ammuneetion."

"In me opeenion thoo're makkin' a fuss aboot noathing onywey," said Henrietta. "If this fella Pottinger comes, all he'll want is for thee tae square up for whit thoo stoll fae his fether."

"I didno steal id, lass," demurred Godfrey uncomfortably. "I cheust took the len' o'd."

"Yaas, withoot askin' for id, an' thoo're niver paid id back."

"No, thoo're no ferly right there. I did pey some o' id back. Ten bob."

"Ten bob," sneered his daughter. "Weel thoo kin pey the rest o'd back when this fella comes. Thoo kin weel afford id noo."

"Yaas, I kin afford id, bit that disno mak' me like id. An' onywey this Pottinger wants me blid. He says id in his letter. An' —"

"Thir's a ker comin' doon the road," interrupted Henrietta.

"Hid's him," yelped Godfrey, and dived behind the girnel.

"Hid's Chohn Clouston o' Quoydunt."

Her father reappeared, looking slightly ashamed of his display of panic.

"He's sheurly comin' here," said Henrietta, "for the ker's stopped at wur gett. He's blawin' his horn too. Thoo'll better awey oot an' see whit he wants."

"Deshed nuisance," muttered Godfrey, but, emerging from behind the girnel, he unlocked and unbolted the door, and ambled down to the gate. He was almost there when he observed that Chohn Clouston was not alone in the car. In the back seat was an unkan individual, but though Godfrey had never set eyes on him before, he knew instantly who it was. The resemblance was unmistakable. That lantern jaw, those narrow, close-set eyes could belong only to the son of Rupert Pottinger. Godfrey stopped dead in his tracks.

"Come awey, boy," said Chohn Clouston impatiently. "Whit er thoo hingin' back for? This is a viseetor for thee. I met him on the road an' he asked whar thee hoose wur, so I gied him a lift. Dis thoo ken whar he is? He's a son o' Rupert Pottinger whar yeused tae work for thee."

Noah Pottinger got out of the car, and advanced to the gate. He was tall, raw-boned, and sun-tanned, and his eyes, as they rested on the veteran of Mucklegutter, held no cordiality.

"Weel," said Chohn Clouston, "a'll be gettan on. Cheerio, Maister Pottinger."

Godfrey came to life. "Wett, Chohn," he screamed. "Stey here. Dinno go awey. This fella's comed tae murder me."

Chohn gaped at him as if he had not heard aright. Then he grinned. "Boy, Godfrey, thoo're me chester. The son o' an ould freend comed tae murder thee. Wett till I tell Chessie yin." And, chuckling heartily, Chohn drove off, reflecting, at the same time, that old Godfrey had a peculiar sense of humour.

○○○○○○

Noah Pottinger and Godfrey confronted one another at the gate.

"Weel, thoo swindlin' ould whalp," said Pottinger. "A'm here."

Godfrey had difficulty in finding words, a highly unusual state for him. He mumbled something about it's being a fine day, and began to back rapidly up the path to the house. Pottinger, advancing after him with equal rapidity, said: "Thoo'll ken whit a'm here for?"

A shudder of apprehension shook the veteran.

"Thoo kinno deu id," he said thickly. "Thoo'll no get awey wi'd. This is no Austrellia. Thir's a laa here, an' if thoo murder me thoo'll heng."

Noah Pottinger made a contemptuous gesture.

"A'm no gaun tae murder thee, thoo ould gappus, though id's whit thoo desserve. I cheust pat yin in me letter tae frighten the wits fae thee."

Godfrey's face cleared slightly. "Thoo—thoo're no gaun tae murder me?"

"Not I. Thoo'll be deid seun enough. A'm comed for the money thoo stoll fae me fether."

Now that he found his life was not in danger, Godfrey regained some of his customary composure. He ushered Pottinger into the farmhouse with a wave of his hand.

"I widno say I stoll the money fae thee fether, boy, bit come in an' wae'll discuss id. Hoo is thee fether onywey?"

"He's deid," said Pottinger curtly.

"Boy, boy, a'm sorry tae hear yin."

"Thoo're sorry like. Bit afore he passed awey he telt me all aboot the wey thoo swindled him oot o' his life savin's. Thoo stoll the hunder an' fifty pound he wur saved tae buy a ferm, an' pat id on a horse, an' lost id, an' niver gied him a cent back."

"I wur herd up at the time, bit I did pay him back some o' id litter."

"Yaas, ten bob. Thoo forced him tae leave Orkney, an' emeegrett tae Austrellia, an' he hid a gey herd time o'd workin' in the mines an' herdly makkin' enough tae bring up his femly. Hooiver, he did weel in the latter end, an' when he passed awey he wur worth a hunder thoosand pounds."

Godfrey's eyes almost popped from his head. "A hunder thoo— Boy, is that true?"

Pottinger nodded.

"My giddy geud," gasped the veteran, "in that case gaun

tae Austrellia wur the best thing he iver did, an' he hid me tae thank for id."

"In a wey," agreed Noah Pottinger, "bit he niver forgave thee for daein' him oot o' his hunder an' fifty pound, an' he swore he widno let thee aff wi' id, bit wid come back tae Orkney an' get id fae thee afore he keeked the bucket. Weel, unfortunately, he niver got the chance, bit I said I wid dae'd for him. So—a'm here, an' thoo kin cheust cough up."

Godfrey eyed him broodingly.

"I suppose thoo'll be weel aff theesel?"

"Oh yaas. Me fether left me a gold mine, an' sixty thoosand pound."

"An' yet thoo're comed all the wey fae Austrellia tae mak' a peur old man pey back a misserable hunder an' fifty pound that I got a len o' forty 'ear ago."

"That thoo stoll forty 'ear ago. Yaas, id's a metter o' principle, thoo sees. Niver let a swindler git awey wi'd. An' come wi' less aboot bein' a peur ould fermer. Maister Clouston o' Quoydunt wur tellin' me thoo're made a packet o' money fae this Government subsidies start. So I want me money, an' I want id queek."

"An' whit if I dinno gie thee id?"

"A'll go tae the polis an' charge thee wi' the theft o' id," snapped Pottinger, his face darkening.

"Thoo couldno prove id."

"Could I no?" Pottinger tapped his coat pocket. "I hiv the letters thoo wrote tae me fether when he wur in Birsay an' Sooth Ronaldshay. Thir's plenty eveedence in them."

The master of Mucklegutter sighed wearily. He knew when he was beaten. "Boy boy, Noah, thoo're a herd case. Shylock wur niver in id wi' the Pottingers." He raised his voice and called, "Henrietta."

His daughter, who had been hovering in the other room, listening anxiously for sounds of violence, and ready, if such should occur, to get her push-bike and ride hell-for-leather for Police Constable Timothy Cursiter, came in.

"Go up the stairs, lass," said her father in heavy tones, "An tak' doon me money box. The wan wi' the twenty-pound notts."   o o o o o o o

"Whar wis yin?" asked Pottinger when Henrietta had gone on her errand.

"Me dowter, Henrietta."

"Me fether niver telt me noathing aboot thee haein' a dowter."

"I mairried again efter he gied tae Austrellia."

"Shae's no bed-like," said Pottinger.

"Shae's a yap o' dirt," grunted Godfrey. "Shae'll be plazed that a'm peyin' thee this money, for shae wur right wild when I telt her aboot me yeusin' thee fether's savin's."

"That shaws on shae his mair honesty than thee. Shae'll be mairried, no doot?"

"A weedow. Shae lost her man in the war. He wur itten be a shark."

"Boy boy," said Pottinger. "It's aye best," and he glanced pointedly at Godfrey, "tae keep weel clear o' sharks, as me peur fether fand oot ower litt."

Henrietta came in with the money box, and placed it on her father's knee. Godfrey opened it with a glum face, disclosing a mass of tightly packed notes.

"Cheust a peur ould fermer, eh?" commented Pottinger sarcastically.

"Hed oot thee hands," grunted the veteran, and he began to count, in a voice that was like the tolling of a passing bell. When he stopped counting, Pottinger, who had been following the proceedings closely, observed, "Yin's cheust £140."

"Thoo'll no alloo a grain o' discoont?" groaned Godfrey.

"No wen happenny. Be rights thoo shid be peyin' interest, bit a'll let thee off wi' hid."

Godfrey produced his wallet, and with a face like a gargoyle counted out a further £9 10s. Pottinger rolled up the wad with a business-like air, snapped a rubber band on it and put it in his pocket. "Weel," he said, "that's that." Godfrey, sunk in gloom, said nothing.

"Thoo'll tak' a gless o' home brew, Maister Pottinger?" inquired Henrietta.

"I will hid," said Pottinger, giving her an approving look. "A'm niver tisted Orkney home brew, bit a'm aften hard me fether spickan aboot id."

Old Ritch looked up with a howl of rage. "Whit's that Henrietta? By geud, a'll no stend for this though. Yin blidsooker's hin a hunder an' forty-nine pound ten fae me, an' he's no gettan me deshed home brew as weel. Stey awey fae yin press."

"Stoop, fether," said Henrietta reprovingly. "All that Maister Pottinger is got fae thee wur his own money, or at laest his fether's. Id wid be an aafil chob if wae let Maister Pottinger go back to Austrellia withoot a tist o' home brew."

Godfrey muttered something to the effect that he would like to give Pottinger a glass of home brew with arsenic in it, but his daughter ignored him, and going to the press brought out a bottle and a glass. Pottinger followed her movements closely and with a thoughtful look in his eye.

"I wur cheust sayin' tae thee fether," he remarked, "that thoo're a weel-like lass. I suppose thoo'll hiv plenty o' admirers."

"Geud, if I hiv," returned Henrietta with a coy titter, "they're aafil carefil no tae tell me."

"Id wur an aafil peety aboot thee man," said Pottinger.

"Not id," said Henrietta, "he wur cheust a dirt."

Pottinger raised his glass. "Here's lukkin' at thee," he said, and drank deeply. He smacked his lips. "Desh, yin wur geud," he observed. "Whar made this?"

"I made it mesel, of coorse," replied Henrietta.

"Id's right deshed geud. A lass like thee desserves a geud hussband."

Henrietta simpered. "Bit whar will I git wen?" she asked roguishly, but with a keen glance at the visitor.

"A'm no mairried mesel," said Pottinger casually.

"That disno surprise me wen bit," put in Godfrey viciously. "I kinno imagine ony lass takkin' thee."

"Tak' no notteece o' me fether," said Henrietta hastily. "He's dottan."

"Desh thee impeedence," roared Godfrey. "Dottan indeed. Thoo're workin' for a right skelp on the lug, Henrietta Kirkness."

"No," went on Pottinger, disregarding the interruption, "a'm no mairried, bit thir's mony an Austrellian lass been efter me."

The Australian visitor tasted the home brew and smacked his lips. "Desh, this is geud," he said. "Whar made it?"

"Thir no herd tae plaze in Austrellia sheurly." This from Godfrey.

"Bit a'm always thowt tae mesel, if I mairry id'll be an Orkney lass. A lass," Pottinger glanced at his empty glass, "whar kin mak' home brew like this, an' whar kin mak' bere bannocks an' sooan scones."

Henrietta got up quickly and replenished his glass.

"Me sooan scones is the best in the pairish," she said, "if I dae say id mesel, an' me bere bannocks is next tae Chessie Clouston's."

Noah Pottinger nodded his head as if this information pleased him. He drained his glass, declined the offer of another, and stood up. "A'll hiv tae be gaun noo," he said, "bit a'll be seein' thee litter on, Mrs Kirkness. An' thanks for the home brew."

"Id's me home brew," snarled Godfrey.

"Id's been right fine tae meet thee, Maister Pottinger," said Henrietta, "an'—"

"Call me Noah," suggested Pottinger.

Henrietta simpered. "Weel, cheerio—Noah, an' I hopp a'll be seein' thee afore thoo go awey."

"Feth, thoo will hid, Mrs Kirkness."

"Thoo kin call me Henrietta, if thoo like."

"I dae like—Henrietta."

"Thoo're aafil Orkney spockan for an Austrellian, Noah," said Henrietta. "Whit wey is yin?"

"Me fether browt me up tae spick noathing bit Orcadian. Weel, cheerio cheust noo, Henrietta."

"Cheerio, Noah."

Pottinger gave Godfrey a glance. "I wid like tae spick tae thee a meenit afore I go, Maister Ritch."

Godfrey followed him sullenly to the gate. "Id's a geud chob," he said, "that thoo didno call me be me first neem, or I wid hiv clashed thee on the mooth wi' me staff. Weel, whit is id?"

"Id's this wey, Maister Ritch. I wur thinkan I wid like tae mairry thee dowter."

Godfrey recoiled with a roar. "Whit? Weel thoo kin think again. My geud goad, thoo come here an' tak' me money, an' then me home brew an' noo thoo want tae tak' me dowter. Clear fae here afore I loss control o' mesel'. Thoo deshed blid-sooker indeed. Afore I wid hiv a Pottinger for a son-in-laa I wid cut me throt. Get oot, an' if I see thee aboothands wi' this ferm again in the time thoo're here a'll tak' me shotgun an' blaw the livin' daylights fae thee."

Pottinger shrugged his shoulders. "Weel," he said, "I thowt I wid ask thee, the wey thoo're her fether, bit no doot Henrietta kin mak' up her mind hersel. I hiv plenty tae offer her, an' no doot shae'll be gled tae git away fae an ould gappus like thee."

He turned and sauntered down towards the road, while Godfrey watched him, scowling. Suddenly the veteran's expression changed.

"Wett a meenit, Pottinger," he cried, and started in pursuit.

"Weel?" queried the Australian.

"Pottinger," said Godfrey, "a'm been thinkin' ower thee suggestion, an' a'm no ferly against id. The warst is, a'm an ould man, an' if Henrietta goes awey wi' thee tae Austrellia whar's gaun tae luk efter me?"

"Thoo could come wi' iss," replied Pottinger, but he said it with a marked absence of enthusiasm.

"Not I begoad," cried Godfrey, "I widno laeve Orkney at me time o' life, an' tae stey wi' a Pottinger aboave all. Na na. Thoo kin tak' me dowter, bit thoo'll need tae gie me some compensession."

"Whit wid thoo call compensession?" inquired Pottinger.

"A hunder," said Godfrey, "an' forty-nine pound ten."

Pottinger's eyes narrowed, and he looked at Godfrey for a long time. Then, with the words, "Swindler is no the neem for id," he reached into his pocket. For the second time that afternoon the sum of £149 10s changed hands.

o o o o o o

Half an hour after this Godfrey sat at the gate of the farm, a jug of home brew in his hand, and on his face a smile that could only have been wider if his ears had been set further back on his head. On the skyline Drydivot's bull still paced to and fro, bogling moodily.

"Bogle awey, boy. Bogle awey," said Godfrey. Dry-divot's bull might have its worries at the moment, but Godfrey had none. He had saved his hundred and forty-nine pounds, and shortly he was going to get rid of the daughter whose presence at Mucklegutter had been a pain in the neck to him for years. Soon Henrietta would be on the other side of the globe, making Noah Pottinger rue the day he had ever set foot in Stenwick.

Godfrey tool a deep and satisfying draught from his jug, and sucked his streaming whiskers. It was a lovely afternoon, and there were even lovelier afternoons to come.

Nobody loves a fat girl

The film was over and the audience began streaming out of the Stenwick Parish Hall, buzzing with comment, some of it appreciative, some not, for as always there were two schools of thought on the standard of the entertainment, the one holding that it had been wonderful, the other taking the view that it had been a lot of bruck.

One of those who inclined to the former view was Jeanick Budge of Snortquoy, who, as she took the arm of her sweetheart, Peedie Tam of Quoydunt, for the walk home, poured out a paean of praise regarding the picture which would have made the Warner Brothers, had they been within earshot, crow with delight.

"My, Tam," she enthused, "is yin Humphrey Bogart no winderfil? Dis thoo ken, I think I wid rether hiv him than Errol Flynn yet. The only wen I didno like in the picture wur yin lass. Whit is this they call her again?"

Peedie Tam looked down at her. "Chinger Rogers, dis thoo mean?" he inquired sharply.

"Whit a daft neem," said Jeanick with a giggle. "I kinno stend her."

"Whit's wrang wi' her?" asked Tam coldly.

"Weel, luk hoo skinny shae is. Mighty, a man wid sheurly niver fall for a lass as skinny as yin."

"I niver thowt shae wur skinny," said Peedie Tam. "I thowt shae wur cheust right."

"Whit a nonsense," tittered Jeanick, squeezing his arm tolerantly. "Thoo couldno possibly like a lass as thin as yin. Id's a winder they pat her in a picture, for thoo could herdly see her side on. Shae wis cheust like a shedda."

Tam glanced at her again, with a peculiar expression on his face.

"Weel weel, Cheanick," he observed, in a tone that was not far removed from a sneer, "nobody kin say thoo're a shedda."

"No, they kinno—" began Jeanick, and then, as she caught the significance of the remark, she stopped. "Whit dis thoo mean, boy? Thoo sheurly widno like tae see me as thin as yin lass, wid thoo?"

"I wid like tae see thee a bit thinner than thoo er, onywey," was her fiance's curt reply.

Jeanick turned over this statement in her mind for a moment.

"Thoo dinno mean tae say thoo think a'm fat?" she cried indignantly. She drew her arm out of his, noting with a pang that he made no attempt to prevent her.

"Thoo're no exactly fat—yet," said Tam, "bit id'll no be lang if thoo're no carefil. Thoo're been pittan on an aafil lot o' weight this peedie while."

"Whit a nonsense," retorted Jeanick, but she said it without conviction. Now that the matter was drawn to her attention she had to admit that her clothes seemed to be getting increasingly tight for her, and that the water in the bath seemed to rise higher up the sides when she went into it.

"Id's no nonsense," said Tam. "A'm notteeced id, a'll tell thee. When thoo yeused tae sit on me knee I herdly could tell thoo wur there, bit noo—"

"Noo whit?"

"Noo me legs is ferly numb afore thoo're been sittin' ten meenits. If thoo dinno watch theesel, thoo'll be as fat as a pallack. Or as fat as thee sister Bella," he added.

"Mercy, Bella's no fat."

"If shae's no fat shae'll deu till somebody fat comes aboothands."

"Mansie disno think shae's fat."

"Whit Mansie thinks is no concern o' mine. Maybe Mansie likes fat lasses. I dinno."

Jeanick stared at him, her lips quivering. So it was out at last. Now she knew the reason for the critical glances Tam had been giving her lately, the increasing reluctance to prolong his visits to Snortquoy, his growing aversion to taking her on his knee and cuddling her as he used to.

Forcing a laugh which rang hollowly in the quiet evening

she prodded him in the ribs and said, "Boy thoo're a right chester, pullin' me leg like yin."

Peedie Tam did not laugh. He met her eyes stonily.

"A'm no been pullin' thee leg, although," he added, with a flash of wry humour, "id could maybe dae wi' pullin' tae thin id oot. Thoo're gittin' fat, Cheanick."

Jeanick's heart dropped into the soles of her dainty shoes. Tears came to her eyes, and at the sight of them Peedie Tam's heart smote him. Producing his handkerchief he moved to her solicitously, but she pushed him violently in the chest, so that he staggered and almost fell, though even as he did so it crossed his mind that the Jeanick of six months or so before could not have pushed with as much beef as that.

"Go awey fae me," sobbed Jeanick. "A'll go home the rest o' the wey mesel."

"Noo noo, lass," said Tam awkwardly, "dinno tak' the poots. A'll tak' the—"

But Jeanick broke away, and made off up the road at a stumbling run, pausing only once to turn and burst out viciously: "Cheust go tae thee Chinger Rogers."

Peedie Tam stood irresolute, wondering whether he ought to go after her and make it up, but just then Jeanick was outlined against the moonlight. She looked like a young heifer. Shrugging his shoulders, Tam remained where he was. There was no doubt about it, Jeanick was getting fat, and he could not abide fat girls.

o o o o o o

In the farmhouse kitchen at Snortquoy, Mrs Budge, Veronica, the Quoydunt landgirl, Bella Budge, and Mansie, the grieve of Quoydunt, were just finishing their regular Tuesday night game of whist. Veronica and Mrs Budge preferred bridge, but Mansie is too thick in the head for bridge. Willie Budge, the master of the house, reclined in a straw-backed chair, feasting his eyes on a line in the County Show issue of the *Orkney Herald* which ran: "Two-year-old heifers in milk or in calf—1, 2, 3, 4 and 5 W. Budge,

Snortquoy, Stenwick." It had been Willie's finest hour, and every night since, he had unfolded the paper to read the line and savour anew the pride of his achievement.

"Weel," said Mrs Budge, getting up reluctantly from the card table, "I suppose id's time I wur pittin' on the supper. Cheanick an' Peedie Tam will be back fae the pictures in a peedie while."

The word were scarcely out of her mouth when footsteps sounded outside, and Jeanick burst in. Throwing her hat on the floor, she ran across the room, flung herself into an armchair, and began sobbing as if her heart would break.

There was consternation in the kitchen; consternation, that is, in all but Willie, who merely looked up irritably from his paper, and demanded: "Whit's shae boglin' aboot?"

Mrs Budge dashed to the side of her weeping daughter.

"Whit's wrang wi' thee, lass. Tell me. An' whar's Peedie Tam?"

Jeanick raised a tear-stained face. "I—I ran awey fae him. A'm feenished wi' him. He—he says a'm ower—ower f-f-f-fat." And laying her head on the arm of the chair she started howling afresh.

In a few minutes, soothed by a cup of tea, she told the whole story.

Mrs Budge's eyes blazed with indignation. "The whalp," she snorted. "The deshed whalp indeed. Thoo're no fat, Cheanick. Thoo're no near as fat as Bella."

"A'm no fat," snapped Bella angrily.

"Thoo er so fat," muttered Jeanick. "An' Tam said I wid seun be as fat as thee."

"I wish he wur here cheust noo," gritted Bella. "He wid git a geud lugget fae me. Fat indeed. A'm no fat, am I Mansie?"

"Geud, thoo're no exactly a skineemelink," replied Mansie with a grin, "bit whit's the differ? I like a fat lass mesel." He recoiled with a yell of protest as his fiancee dealt him a crisp skelp on the side of the head.

"That's for sayin' a'm fat," she snapped.

"Whar's fat?" inquired Willie Budge at this point, with mild interest.

His wife informed him of the situation, and Willie subjected his younger daughter to a thoughtful scrutiny.

"Weel, thoo're no whit I wid call fat mesel," he announced, "bit thir's no doot thoo're a piece heavier aboot the behind than thoo wur."

"Id's a lie," wailed Jeanick.

"Id's no a lie," replied Willie calmly. "Thoo're certainly gittan plumper, Tam wur right enough there. I widno obchect tae id mesel, for a'm like Mansie. I like lasses tae be weel covered, so that thoo kin hiv something tae grip. Lockars, when I wur coortin' thee mither shae wur like a young elephant."

"Whit a doonright lie, Willie Budge."

"Thoo kin tak a luk at some o' yin ould phottagraphs if thoo dinno believe id," answered Willie with a shrug. "Bit as I wur sayin', I dinno obchect tae fat weemin. Tam eveedently thinks different." And with that Willie took up his paper again, and washed his hands of the conversation, in which he was not greatly interested in any case. Fat cattle, yes. He could talk on that subject with considerable animation. But fat weemin, no.

Mrs Budge appealed to Veronica. "Wid thoo say Cheanick wur ower fat?"

"Frankly, no," replied the landgirl. "I'd say she is just nicely plump at the moment, but she will be fat if she keeps putting on weight at the rate she is doing. If I were you, Jeanick, I'd cut down on these buttered scones. You've eaten six since you came in."

Jeanick, with a seventh scone half way to her mouth, looked at it guiltily, and after a slight struggle with herself, laid it down.

"I dinno see whit wey I shid sterve mesel cheust tae seut Tam," she said sullenly. "If he disno want me thir's plenty whar dis."

"Feth, thoo're right there, Jeanick," her mother backed her up. "Humphrey Bews wid tak' thee in a meenit, fat or no fat."

"Dinno keep spickan as though I wur fat," said Jeanick peevishly. "Yaas, Humphrey wid chump at the chance o' gaun wi' me. He wur right wild when Tam did him oot."

"But it's Tam you love, isn't it?" put in Veronica.

Jeanick tossed her head. "I kin dae wantin' him," she said. "If he wid rether hiv Chinger Rogers he kin tak' her."

"Whar is this Rogers lass, onywey?" inquired Mrs Budge. "I ken nobody o' that neem in Stenwick. Shae's sheurly unkan."

"Shae's a film ster, mither," explained Bella impatiently. "Shae wur in the film whit wur on in the hall the night."

"An' whit wey dis Tam ken her?" asked Mrs Budge, who is a little slow on the uptake at times.

"He disno ken her," snapped Jeanick. "Shae's in Amereeca. He's niver seen her except on the films. All shae his tae deu wi' this is that I said tae Tam shae wur ower thin, an' then he got on aboot me bein' fat."

"I mind a Rogers fella," remarked Willie, without looking up from his paper, "whar chudged Shorthorn coos at the Dounby Show wen 'ear afore the war. Osswald Rogers, his neem wis. Wid hid be the sam' Rogers?"

"No," said Bella.

"Weel weel," said Willie indifferently. "Id disno metter."

"Chinger Rogers or no Chinger Rogers," said Mrs Budge spiritedly, "Peedie Tam's a gappus if he thinks thoo're fat, Cheanick. Noo, tak' up yin ither scone if thoo want id, an' dinno let Tam pit thee aff thee appeetite. I like tae see lasses whar kin tak' thir maet. Tam'll likely be here the morn as yeusual, feelin' sorry for the wey he's behaved."

"He disno need tae bother," snorted Jeanick, taking her mother's advice and falling upon the scone like a hungry python.

○ ○ ○ ○ ○ ○

Veronica went down to Quoydunt about an hour after this and found Peedie Tam in the kitchen moodily playing his mouth-organ, to the annoyance of his employer, Chohn Clouston, who was trying to listen to the wireless.

"Well," she said severely, "you've done it this time. Jeanick's in a fine state."

Chessie Clouston dropped her knitting, and gave Peedie Tam a horrified stare.

"My mercy, boy," she gasped, "whit er thoo deun? Thoo're no—?"

"It's all right, Mrs Clouston," said Veronica with a laugh, "It's not as serious as that. They've only quarrelled."

Chessie sighed with relief.

"Geud, thoo made me go weck. So thir fowt, er they? I windered whit Tam wur back so early for. Whit er thoo fowt aboot, boy?"

Peedie Tam glanced at her sullenly, and went on playing his mouth-organ.

"Tam told her she was getting too fat, and left her. Poor Jeanick come home nearly broken-hearted," explained the landgirl.

Tam laid down his mouth-organ, "So shae is gettan fat," he grunted, "bit I didno laeve her. Shae left me. I cheust telt her for her own geud, bit shae ran awey boglin' like a bull. Weel, if that's the wey shae wants id, id seuts me, for I kinno be daein' wi' fat lasses."

"But it's not the way she wants it," said Veronica. "She's hurt and she's angry, but she still loves you. If I were you I'd go right up to Snortquoy this minute, and put your arms round her and say you're sorry."

"Pit me erms roond her," sneered Tam. "That's a geud wen. Me erms'll no go roond her noo. An' onywey I hiv noathing tae be sorry for. I telt her the truth, an' shae didno like id, an' took the poots."

"Dinno be so stickit, boy," snapped Chessie. "Cheust thoo dae as Veronica says, an' go an' mak' id up. Tellan the lass shae wur fat indeed. I niver hard the like. Shae's no fat."

Tam shrugged his shoulders. "That's thee opeenion. I think different. If shae'll go on diet, an' get her weight doon a'll go back, bit except shae dis hid a'm feenished." He glanced keenly at Veronica. "A'll swear shae made a right herty supper when shae cam' home, brocken-hearted or no, did shae?"

Veronica looked a little confused.

"Well," she admitted, "her appetite didn't seem to be much affected."

"I thowt hid," said Tam, and picked up his mouth-organ as an indication that as far as he was concerned there was no more to be said.

Chohn Clouston switched off the wireless with a snort of disgust.

"That's the news deun, an' I herdly hard a word o' id for the hulleeballoo thoo wur all keekin' up. Whit's all this aboot somebody bein' ower fat? Id's no thee sheurly Veronica?"

"Certainly not," said the landgirl indignantly. "We're talking about Jeanick Budge of Snortquoy."

"Lockars, is shae gotten fat? I kinno say a'm notteeced id, bit of coorse a'm no seen the lass for a peedie while. Id's funny the wey some weemin's fat an' some is thin."

"The same can be said of all God's creatures," observed Veronica.

"Yaas, maybe thoo're right, bit somehoo or ither thoo notteece id more wi' weemin. Er thoo notteeced id, Tam?"

"I am hid," replied Peedie Tam, with some emphasis.

"In some femlies," proceeded Chohn, warming to his theme, "all the weemin' is fat, an' in ither femlies thir all skinny. Tak' the Budges noo. Delphine Budge is a gret clash o' a wife, an her mither wur the sam' an' when thoo tell me Cheanick is gaun the sam' wey a'm no wen bit surprised. Spickan aboot Delphine Budge, I mind wen night when Willie wur coortin' her—"

"Chohn," broke in his wife coldly, for she had heard this anecdote before.

"Whit? Oh weel, niver mind," finished Chohn lamely. "Maybe the less said aboot id the better, indeed." He rose and put on his cap, and went out with the announcement that he was going to have a look at his great bull Bluebell, the apple of his eye, before going to bed.

"So you're not going to make it up with Jeanick?" Veronica challenged Peedie Tam.

"Not I feth," was the reply. "Shae's made her bed, an' noo shae min lie in id. If," he added, with a touch of mordant humour, "the bed'll hed up under her weight."

○ ○ ○ ○ ○ ○

Both Veronica and Chessie Clouston expected that, after a night's sleep, Tam would think better of his decision, and make haste to soothe Jeanick's feelings and heal the breach in the romance, for they had been going together for a long time now, and their affection for one another was deeply rooted. Tam did, in fact, appear the following morning with a thoughtful air, and the general expression of one in whom the pangs of remorse were busily at work, and he did, shortly after breakfast, start off to walk in the direction of Snortquoy. On the way there he met Jeanick face to face. They stopped, and there was an awkward silence. Tam cleared his throat, preparatory to saying, "A'm aafil sorry aboot last night, lass. Will thoo tak' me back?" but before the remark could be uttered, Jeanick, smarting with wounded pride, shot out: "My, I thowt thoo wid be awey efter thee Chinger Rogers be this time."

Peedie Tam stepped back, his eyes hardening.

"Thoo'll better go back tae Quoydunt," pursued Jeanick, "for thoo'll no find her up this wey."

"Righto Fatty," gritted Tam, and turning his back on her he strode off at a rapid pace. If his pace had been less rapid, and his boots had made less noise on the stony road, he would have heard Jeanick's broken cry of "Tam, Tam, I didno mean id." As it was he did not hear it, and reached Quoydunt seething, and swearing that that was the feenish between him and Jeanick Budge.

As for Jeanick she waited in the road for a while, hoping that Tam would turn back, sweep her into his arms, and cover her face with burning kisses, but as Tam walked swiftly on and eventually disappeared behind one of the outhouses of Quoydunt, she herself slowly retraced her steps to Snortquoy. Womanlike, she did not consider that it was her own hostile greeting of Tam that had wrecked the set-up for a reconciliation. Tam, in her view, should have allowed her to vent her spleen, laughed it off, and then folded her in an affectionate embrace. Instead he had replied with a contemptuous taunt, ignored her olive branch, and left her standing in the road like a geup. In fact he had tossed her aside like a worn-out glove.

Jeanick was unfamiliar with the statement of the poet

that "Hell hath no fury like a woman scorned", but if anyone had drawn it to her attention she would have commented that the writer knew what he was talking about. All the way home to Snortquoy fury fermented in her ample bosom like potatoes bubbling in a pot, and by the time she stepped into the farmhouse her only regret was that she had let Tam away without a really juicy cloor on the lug.

She was in a venomous mood when Veronica arrived shortly afterward with the information that Tam was willing to take her back provided she went on diet and brought her weight down.

"Go on diet indeed," she cried. "The deshed whalp, a'll see him fer enough afore I go on ony diet. An' thoo kin tell him fae me that even if I shid get thin—no that a'm sayin' a'm fat—id'll be for no yeuse tae him tae come craalin' back tae me. An' thoo kin gie him this."

And with these spirited words Jeanick wrenched off her engagement ring which Peedie Tam had slipped on a considerably slimmer finger eighteen months before, and handed it to the landgirl.

Tam received the ring at tea time with an expressionless face, and placed it in his waistcoat pocket with the comment: "Weel, that's iss ferly feenished noo."

○ ○ ○ ○ ○ ○

The breaking of the engagement, and more particularly the reason for it, was discussed widely in the parish during the next few days, and varied views were expressed, some of which roundly condemned Tam's behaviour in the matter, while others just as staunchly upheld it. The view of the latter school of thought was well expressed by old Godfrey Ritch of Mucklegutter, who, over a glass of home brew in the farmhouse of Drydivot, stated: "Desh, if a fella disno want a fat wife he's justeefied in tellin' her, an' if the lass disno tak' steps tae get her weight doon shae kinno compleen if shae losses him. Efter thir married, of corse, id's a different storry, for as thoo're aware, a man tak's his wife for better or for warse—chenerally id's warse—an' if shae gets fat thir's noathing he kin dae, except maybe gie her a geud skelp noo an' again cheust tae shaw her he disno approve o' her bein' fat. For mesel I think Tam is makkin' a fuss aboot noathing. A'm hin experience o' a fat wife an' a thin wife, an' the both o' them wis bizzoms. Me first wife wur as fat as a heystack, an' when shae keeked the bucket I thowt I wid like a change, so I mairried a lass whar wis as thin as a sterved rat. In me opeenion id mak's little difference if a wife is fat or thin as long as shae keeps her mooth shut, an' dis whit shae's telt, an' kin mak' geud home brew, bit a'm come tae the conclusion, in me ould age, that id's fer the best tae hiv no wife at all."

By and large the male population of the parish supported Peedie Tam, and in a good many farmhouses the controversy had domestic repercussions, as farmers began to cast jaundiced eyes on their broad-beamed spouses and make sarcastic comments about frocks that were prone to split down the back and skirts that would not button round the middle, and open up old pre-nuptial snapshot albums and brood over the sylph-like figures their wives had once possessed.

As for the females of Stenwick, not all of them backed up Jeanick. The younger daughter of Snortquoy had the sympathy only of those of her sex, who, like herself, were putting on flesh. Stenwick girls of slender, not to say emaciated, outline, considered that what Peedie Tam had done was only right and proper, and expressed surprise at his not having parted brass rags with Jeanick before. There were a few, such as Mercedes Garson, Delilah Bews, and Jezebel Flett, who reasoned that if Tam was repelled by an obese lass he would naturally be attracted by a weedy one, and they began to take every opportunity of thrusting themselves into Tam's company. Mercedes started to take an absorbed interest in Quoydunt's new tractor, which Tam normally operates. Delilah, more subtle, bribed her young brother to remark, in Tam's hearing, that Delilah's waist measurement was identical with that of Ginger Rogers. Jezebel, not subtle at all, accosted Tam outside the Post Office one afternoon and with a bright smile suggested that she was available for marriage if Tam wanted her, a suggestion to which Tam turned a deaf ear, for Jezebel's slimness is without a redeeming curve; seen in silhouette she closely resembles a plank.

Meanwhile Jeanick found her confident belief that Humphrey Bews would be delighted to re-establish himself on the old footing as her sweetheart very much wide of the mark. Humphrey had certainly accepted an invitation to tea, but he had looked at her askance several times during the meal, and when afterwards she had coyly reminded him that there was a sofa in the best room where they would not be interrupted, he had shown himself ill at ease, and had excused himself on the grounds that he had to go home and repair a dung-spreader. Jeanick, aware that the Bews dung-spreader had been in Geordie Manson's smiddy for the past week, and recognising a brush-off when she received one, had coldly bidden him goodnight, concealing her chagrin as best she could. She learned later from Mrs Manson of the Post Office that Humphrey, calling there for cigarettes on the way home, had expressed himself in terms unflattering to herself, saying that he had liked her when she had wen chin, bit no noo when shae hid three.

At the end of a week the rift in the lute was as wide as ever, and it began to look to the parish as though it was going to be permanent. Neither Peedie Tam nor Jeanick looked very happy about this state of affairs. Tam, never a particularly loquacious individual, sank into sullen taciturnity, toyed with his food, and went to the bothy he shared with Mansie early in the evenings, there to sit on his bed playing doleful music on his mouth-organ for hours at a stretch. Jeanick became snappish and short-tempered and developed a tendency to fly off the handle for the slightest reason, and even for no reason at all. One evening, for instance, after sitting watching her father for some time with a brooding look, she stalked over to him, snatched the *Scottish Farmer* out of his hands and tossed it in the fireplace with the angry words, "Thoo're aye readin' yin deshed pipper." The patience of her family was greatly tried, and Willie Budge, for one, cursed the day when Peedie Tam had been so tactless as to tell Jeanick she was getting fat. But, ironically enough, though Jeanick was clearly pining, it made her no slimmer. The more she pined the heartier her appetite grew, and the more spherical her outline became.

She and Peedie Tam avoided one another as much as possible, but when, once or twice, they did meet on the road it was to pass with averted faces and without recognition, though once, Peedie Tam, sitting on a dyke while Jeanick was approaching, could not resist bringing out his mouth-organ and greeting her with the strains of the ditty which goes, "I don't want her, you can have her, she's too fat for me." Jeanick hurried past with a red face and blazing eyes.

○ ○ ○ ○ ○ ○

Peedie Tam was cycling home from Dounby. It was a dark, sultry night about ten days after his quarrel with Jeanick, and of late he had taken to going into Dounby and indulging in drinking sessions with such hardened Stenwick topers as Vernon Isbister and Gregory Scarth. Tam's friends had noted this development with regret. Tristam Mainland warned him that if he kept it up he would be in poor fettle for the next football season, to which Tam had indifferently replied that he intended to give up football in any case. The parish minister had gravely informed him that he was on the road to perdition, to which Tam, with not the clearest of ideas as to what perdition meant, curtly retorted "Id seuts me." Even old Godfrey Ritch, who practically lives on home brewed ale, had been heard to express the view that Tam was going a bit ower fer.

As he rode, Tam was clothed in a pleasant aura of forgetfulness. He leaned well forward over the handlebars, steering somewhat casually with his elbows, and as he rode he hummed snatches of old songs, like Ophelia when she floated to her death in the brook. The alcoholic haze in front of his eyes prevented him seeing where he was going very well, but as he was carrying no lights it did not matter very much. A sudden acceleration in the pace of his machine suggested to him that he had reached the long brae which begins just opposite the ruined croft of Clapshothill.

As Peedie Tam played "She's too fat for me" on his mouth-organ, Jeanick Budge hurried past with head averted.

The bike rushed downward at breakneck speed, weaving crazily from side to side. Warm air whipped past. Exhilarated, Tam sat erect in his seat, swaying, and raised his voice in the rollicking "Kitty Berdo hid a coo." To make his posture more comfortable, he let go the handlebars. The notion crossed his mind, vaguely, that there was a sharp right-hand bend at the foot of this brae. But he was not sure. Perhaps he was thinking of some other brae. "Black an' white aboot the moo," he roared.

o o o o o o

Jeanick Budge, out for an evening walk, and wrapped in a gloomy reverie, became suddenly aware of a crash and a thud somewhere on the road ahead of her, and then silence, broken by the slow whir of a bicycle wheel spinning in the air.

"My mighty," she gasped, "thir's sheurly been an acceedent." She broke into a sharp trot, switching on her plicko and flashing it into the roadside as she ran. Presently she saw the bicycle, lying in the ditch just where the road turned at the foot of the Clapshothill brae, its rear wheel sticking into the air and still turning gently. Of the cyclist there was no sign, but suddenly there was a low moan from beyond the ditch.

Jeanick jumped the ditch, climbed over a barbed wire fence with such rapidity that she left about a square foot of her skirt behind on the strands, and stumbled over something. She flashed her torch downward and a ringing shriek left her lips.

"Tam."

Her ex-fiance lay motionless on the field, his face a waxy yellow in the plicko's ray, and a trickle of blood on his forehead.

Jeanick knelt beside him. "Tam, Tam," she wailed. "Spick tae me. Say thoo're no deid." She leaned over to ascertain if he was breathing. He was breathing all right. The whisky-laden whiff she received made her draw back sharply.

"Tam," she cried, "er thoo bed hurt? Say something, boy."

Tam stirred slightly and groaned. His mouth opened. He said thickly, "Anither three nips, berman."

Jeanick thought desperately. What did one do to bring an unconscious man to his senses? Slosh water in his face? But there was no water aboothands. She slapped him smartly across the cheek, and again Tam opened a bleary eye.

"Whar's hittan me?" he demanded irritably. "Wett till I—"

"Tam, this is me, thee own peedie Cheanick."

"Me Cheanick? Me Cheanick's fer fae peedie, a'll tell thee."

The girl's eyes glittered, but only for a moment. Tam was dazed. He did not know what he was saying. Nevertheless she gave him another juicy smack, just for luck. Tam's other eye opened. Recognition appeared in it.

"Cheanick," he said. "Whit er thoo daein' here? Whit's happened? Whar's Vernon Isbeester an' Gregory Scarth?"

"Thir no here. Thoo're hin an acceedent wi' thee bike. Er thoo muckle hurt?"

"Bes' kens. Me heid's ferly splittan onywey. I shid niver hiv hin yin last three nips."

"A'll try an' help thee up," said Jeanick. She lifted his shoulder, but at the first movement he squealed like a stuck pig.

"I doot thoo're brocken something," faltered Jeanick.

"I think a'm brocken me back," groaned Tam. "An' both me legs. An' I widno be a bit surprised if me skull wurno fractured."

"Oh Tam," gulped Jeanick. It occurred to her that a man with a broken back, two broken legs and a fractured skull was not much use to any girl, but perhaps Tam was exaggerating his injuries. There was only one way of finding out. She got up with decision.

"A'm gaun for the doctor," she said. "Cheust thoo wett here till I come back."

"Feth a'll deu hid," replied Tam wryly. As the girl was about to move away he said hesitantly: "Cheanick, in case me inchuries is fatal, an' I pass awey afore thoo come back, I wid cheust like tae say a'm aafil sorry a'm been bed tae thee. Thoo kinno help gittan fat."

"A'm no—" cut in Jeanick, and stopped. It was no time for an argument.

"Nobody kin help gittan fat," went on Tam. "Id's cheust the wey o' the world, an' a'm sorry I iver cast id up tae thee. Thee engagement ring is in me checket pocket, lass. Will thoo tak' id oot an' pit id on? If a'm gaun tae keek the bucket I wid like tae be engaged tae thee again first."

With tear-dimmed eyes Jeanick fished in his pocket, and among an assortment of beer-bottle corks located the ring. She slipped it on her finger, bent and kissed Tam tenderly, and said, "A'm awey noo."

Bounding over the fence she landed sprawling in the ditch, skinning her chin on the edge of the road. It had been her intention to use Tam's bike for her errand of mercy but as she dragged it out of the ditch she saw that this was out of the question as its front wheel was the shape of a parallelogram. She dropped the useless machine, and set her teeth. There was only one thing for it. At a spanking run she charged forward up the Clapshothill brae.

○ ○ ○ ○ ○ ○

The house of Dr Harvey Crippen, Stenwick's unhappily-named medical man, was about three miles from the scene of Peedie Tam's smash, but to Jeanick, as she steamed along the road, it seemed more like thirteen. As has been stated it was a sultry night, and before she had gone very far Jeanick, who was not particularly lightly clad, was spouting sweat like a burst water-main, but love and anxiety drove her on at a cracking pace. Whenever her steps lagged she pictured Tam expiring in twitches of agony, and gained an immediate acceleration.

By the foulest luck there was no traffic on the road at all, so that though she kept her eyes skinned for the chance of a lift there was nothing doing. At last she reeled up to the door of the doctor's house, and battered on it with a will. Dr Crippen's elderly housekeeper appeared.

"A'm wantin' the doctor," gasped Jeanick. "Thir's been an acceedent."

"He's no in," said the housekeeper. "He gied awey ower tae the ferm o' Pleeps, whar Galahad Davie's wife's haein' a bern, aboot half an 'oor ago."

Jeanick sagged against the wall with a hollow groan. "Whit will I dae?" she wailed. "Kin thoo phone Pleeps an' tell him tae go tae the feet o' Clapshothill brae? Id's urchent."

"Pleeps is no on the phone," said the housekeeper. "Thoo'll better come in an' wett, lass, for thoo're ferly deun."

"I kinno wett," fretted Jeanick. "Could thoo gie me a len' o' a bike?"

"I hivno a bike," was the reply.

Jeanick sighed and braced herself for the inevitable. She threw back her head, took a deep breath, and plugged off in the direction of Pleeps, another three miles distant. There is not the space available, to do justice to Jeanick's nocturnal marathon. At just after midnight she was knocking on the door of Pleeps, only to be told by an exuberant Galahad Davie that the doctor had been and gone, that he had done his stuff nobly, and that, in consequence he, Galahad, was the father of a twelve-pound boy. The drooping Jeanick had protested that the doctor had not returned home or his car would have passed her on the road, and Galahad said that was right, but as a matter of fact the doctor had gone on to the Post Office, where Janet Manson's twins had a joint attack of mumps. Galahad regretted that he could not give Jeanick a lift to the Post Office, as his car was broken down, and he could not leave his wife in any case. He gave Jeanick a glass of sherry however, and wished her the best of luck, and hoped Peedie Tam would be in better shape when she got back to him.

Once again the weary Jeanick hit the trail, at a pace which now resembled the shamble of a paralysed hippopotamus, and at one-thirty was beating a tattoo on the Post Office door. An upstairs window was flung open and Geordie Manson's irate tones demanded; "Whar's makkin' yin deshed hulleebaloo? The berns is sleepin'."

"Whar's the doctor?" shouted Jeanick.

"He's awey fae her a quarter o' an 'oor ago," retorted

Geordie, and slammed the window shut. Jeanick collapsed on the doorstep, and burst into tears. Presently she struggled to her feet. If the doctor had made for home from here he must have gone up the Clapshothill brae. Perhaps he would notice the wrecked bike and stop. Perhaps, by the irony of things, he would drive straight on, unaware that Peedie Tam was dying a few yards away. In any case, Jeanick reflected, there was no rest yet for her. Lurching forward she set off down the road at a floundering stumble.

o o o o o o

By the time she neared the foot of Clapshothill brae Jeanick was in a parlous state. She was falling on her hands and knees at every half dozen steps, steam was rising from her in clouds, her legs were as devoid of flexibility as two pieces of wood, and, as she had lost a shoe some way back, the sole of her right foot was covered with blisters the size of marbles. She gave no thought, however, to her own plight. Her mind was filled to the exclusion of all else with the question, would she find Tam alive, or lying a cold, stiff corpse?

She flashed her plicko into the side of the road. Ah, there was the bike. Then she froze, as a voice came out of the darkness.

"Cheanick, is yin thee, lass? Whar on earth er thoo been all this time?"

Jeanick swung her torch in the direction of the voice. She saw Peedie Tam sitting composedly at the roadside, a cigarette in his mouth, looking a little bored, but otherwise all right.

"Tam," she gasped, staggering towards him, "er thoo better?"

"A'm fine," he replied. "Desh the thing's wrang wi' me, except a peedie cut on me broo, an' the doctor pat a bit o' plester on id."

"The doctor. My mercy a'm been runnin' all ower the pairish lukkin' for him. A'm ferly deun." She reeled into the ditch and lay there gasping.

"Geud secks, lass, I thowt thoo wur sheurly gone home an' forgot aboot me. Yaas, the doctor cam' by in his ker a while ago an' stopped an' hid a luk at me, an' said I wur fine." He stood up. "Weel, I suppose wae'll better start back for Snortquoy."

Jeanick groaned, "Tam, I couldno moave wen step. Thoo'll hiv tae cairry me."

Tam stiffened, "Cairry thee. My mighty, Cheanick, I dinno ken if I kin manage that. Hooiver a'll trey id. Come awey." He assisted her to her feet and swung her up into his arms.

"Geud goad," he exclaimed in amazement, "thoo're as light as a feather. Whit's happened? Gie me the plicko." He set her down and shone the torch on her. His jaw dropped. "My lockers, lass, thoo're ferly thin. Thoo're lost punds an' punds. Id's winderfil."

In spite of her weariness Jeanick's eyes sparkled. She realised what had happened. In her chase of the doctor she had covered nearly ten miles and had lost enough sweat to float the St Ninian.

"Dis thoo think thoo kin cairry me tae Snortquoy, Tam?" she asked coyly.

"Cairry thee. Fine hid." He swept her up again, tossed her in the air, caught her coming down, and kissed her passionately. Then holding her tightly in his arms he set off at a brisk lope towards Snortquoy.

Jeanick clung happily to his neck. Only one thought disturbed her. Could she keep this miraculously regained slimness? Yes, she decided, at all costs she must, even if it meant putting on a couple of heavy sweaters and doing an hour's cross-country running every morning. For a svelte figure no sacrifice was too great.

The Face in the Mirror

Among other things, Stenwick prides itself upon the comeliness of its damsels, but, just as there is no rose without a thorn, so there is no parish whose gallery of feminine pulchritude is utterly flawless. Stenwick is no exception.

The visitor, having viewed with delight the charms of Andromeda Laird of Gutterbogs, Jeanick Budge of Snortquoy, Audrey Craigie of Swashmidden, Medusa Wishart of Mucklebruck, and Drusilla Matches of Quoyraffle, amongst others, is apt to come suddenly upon Chloe Harcus of Rumtodly, of whose face it has been frequently observed that it would stop a clock.

The unfortunate Chloe certainly lacks, to a remarkable degree, all the qualities that go to make a pin-up girl. It is often the case that two unprepossessing parents can produce a beautiful daughter, but in Chloe's case the union of Cuthbert Harcus and Amnesia Moodie had achieved no such miracle. Chloe had inherited the least attractive features of both her father and mother, her father's prognathous jaw, receding forehead, and squinting eyes, her mother's flat nose, sticking out ears, short, dumpy figure, and bow legs. It is not surprising, therefore, that Chloe, at the age of 26, was high and dry upon the shelf.

Perhaps Fate's unkindest cut of all was that after turning out Chloe in so repulsive a mould she had endowed the girl with a romantic and passionate nature. Chloe yearned for love with all the wistful longing of which her heart was capable. She dreamed nightly of being pursued across meadows by handsome young ploughmen who would catch her, sweep her into their arms, and cover her face with burning kisses. In her waking moments she day-dreamed the same thing, but in her day-dreams she did not worry much whether the ploughmen were handsome, or even particularly young. Chloe's attitude was that she would willingly settle for any member of the male sex.

If the impression has been given that Chloe spent her time lamenting her lot, this was far from being the case. Although not possessing much in the way of looks, Chloe had plenty of character, and in the matter of romance she was a confirmed optimist. Sooner or later, she was convinced, love would come along, and when it came she was determined that opportunity would not need to knock twice. In the meantime she waited, with as much patience as she could, and prepared herself for the day.

All that could be done to improve her appearance Chloe had done. Her room was filled with skin ointments, mudpacks, vanishing creams, hair lotions, lip salves, and numerous other cosmetic preparations, and she did not stint herself in their use. She wrote incessantly to magazine advertisers for corrective devices for outstanding ears, bow legs, flat noses, and squint eyes. By quacks in every part of the British Isles she was regarded as the queen of suckers.

Her perseverance went entirely unrewarded. Her skin remained blotchy, her blackheads did not diminish, either in size or in quantity, her nose stayed flat, her eyes squint, her ears outstanding, and her legs bandy. All that happened was that her father's eyes grew a little more bloodshot, and his temper worse. Cuthbert Harcus would have liked nothing better than to get his daughter off his hands, but while he felt that any money devoted to this end was money well spent, he was beginning to feel that the strain on his purse was getting to be a little too much. Just before this story opens, in fact, he had been driven into a fury at having to foot the bill for an expensive mechanism Chloe had ordered for the purpose of curing her bow legs. That it completely failed to cure them made him none the happier.

It may be thought, surely in the parish of Stenwick, or in the surrounding parishes, there was at least one short-sighted, ill-favoured bachelor who would find nothing much to object to in Chloe's appearance. Unfortunately there was among Chloe's shortcomings one which appealed to the ear as little as her looks appealed to the eye. She had no roof to her mouth, with the result that her speech was almost entirely in vowels, and virtually unintelligible except to those schooled to understand her from long practice. Thus the one or two males in the district who were not put off by her face from considering her as a possible spouse, most decidedly jibbed at the idea of linking themselves for life to one whose enunciation resembled that of an irritable sow.

This lengthy, but necessary, preamble over, on to our story.

o o o o o o

Chloe Harcus sat at the dressing-table in her bedroom, staring expectantly into her mirror. It was her birthday, and the time was a minute or two to midnight. She presented an unglamorous picture, in a voluminous nightgown of blue flannel, with her hair in curl papers, her face smeared to a depth of about a quarter of an inch with an ointment highly spoken of by a famous film actress, and with a thing like a clamp screwed to her nose. It was not her reflection, however, that interested Chloe at this time. A day or two ago she had been informed by an old tinkler wife that if a girl looked in a mirror at midnight on her birthday, and repeated a certain incantation, she would see in the glass the face of her future husband. Many disappointments had rendered Chloe somewhat sceptical of these superstitions, but as her birthday was just about due she had decided that there was nothing to be lost by giving it a trial.

Glancing at her watch, she saw that the witching hour was only a couple of seconds away. She leaned forward, cleared her throat, and prepared to pronounce the magic word: "Mirror, mirror, I ask you, show me the face of my husband true."

o o o o o o

Felix Garson looked round him in perplexity, cursing the thick mist which had suddenly come down. Twenty minutes ago he had left home in bright moonlight to pay a nocturnal call on the girl of his heart, Desdemona Hourston of Whassigo, but, well as he knew the way, this infernal mist

had made him lose his bearings completely. He shifted the
ladder he was carrying from one shoulder to the other, while
he looked this way and that for something which would
guide him to his destination. That he was near Whassigo he
was certain, for he had covered nearly half the distance there
before the mist came down.

Suddenly he uttered an exclamation. Ah, there it was, the
faint gleam of a lighted window. That would be the window
of Desdemona's bedroom, for she had promised to leave a
candle burning as a signal that her parents had gone to bed,
and that all was clear. Taking a firm grip of his ladder he
stepped briskly forward, and in a few minutes was standing
under the lighted window, in the gable of a farmhouse.

It occurred to him that the window seemed to have
shifted position a little since he last visited Whassigo a week
or so before. He remembered it as having been more towards
the back of the house, and also a little higher from the
ground. But perhaps Desdemona was now sleeping in a
different bedroom. Cautiously, for he knew that Desdemona's
father, Silas Hourston, was no believer in the good old
Orkney custom of nighting, and that he would meet with
short shrift if caught, he placed his ladder against the wall
and silently began to ascend. He noticed, somewhat to his
annoyance, that Desdemona had neglected to leave the
window open.

He reached the level of the window sill, stepped up
another rung and leaned forward against the pane, peering
into the room, preparatory to drawing Desdemona's
attention to his arrival with a tap. The tap was never made.
Felix froze, with his knuckles poised, and his eyes goggling.
There was someone in the room, sitting back on to him, but
he could see her reflection in the mirror, and it was the
reflection of a face that was scarcely human, a pallid
luminously-gleaming face, with no nose, but a hideous metal
fixing in its place.

"Geud goad," gasped Felix, and came down the ladder at
a breakneck pace. Who this horrible apparition was in
Desdemona's room he did not know, but it certainly was
not Desdemona. Reaching terra firma in a cold sweat he
snatched his ladder away from the wall, tucked it under his

arm, and set out to remove himself from the vicinity of the house with all possible speed. At the front of the house a chain rattled and a dog barked. Felix stopped in surprise. There was no dog at Whassigo. He looked back at the farmhouse. The mist had thinned a little and he could now see the outlines of the building.

"My mighty," he said to himself, "whit a geup a'm been." For this, he now realised, was not Whassigo at all. It was the neighbouring farm of Rumtodly, and the girl into whose bedroom he had nearly intruded had been Chloe Harcus, Chloe with her face laggered with cold cream, and wearing one of the corrective nose attachments with which she was continually experimenting.

Felix laughed heartily at his blunder, but all the same his nerve had been shaken by the incident, and he did not head for Whassigo, but went home. Going to the lasses had no further appeal for him this night.

o o o o o o

Chloe stared wide-eyed at her mirror. It had really happened. Just as the tinkler wife had said. As she had finished pronouncing the incantation there had appeared in the mirror, over her shoulder, clearly and distinctly, a man's face, the face of Felix Garson. It had been visible for only a moment, and then it had vanished as quickly as it had come. There had been no possibility of mistaking its identity. It had been Felix Garson of Burstin all right. True, the expression on the face had been somewhat disappointing. It had not been a tender or romantic look, but rather a look of horrified amazement. Still, Chloe was not disposed to quibble about that. The important fact was that Felix Garson was her future husband.

She could hardly believe her good fortune. Never in her wildest dreams had she imagined that Felix Garson was earmarked as her mate. He fulfilled all the qualifications of her ideal. He was young. He was handsome. He was tall, broad-shouldered and muscular, and he had a smile of singular charm. Furthermore his people were well-off. It was true that for some little time he had been going steady with Desdemona Hourston of Whassigo, but obviously that romance was not destined to get far. What was written in the stars must come true, and it was written in the stars that Felix Garson was to be the husband of Chloe Harcus.

In an access of happiness Chloe leapt from her chair and cavorted about the room, singing, and kicking up her legs, until her father battered angrily on the adjoining wall and bawled: "Whit the dickens dis thoo think thoo're daein', keekin' up yin hulleebaloo at this time o' the night? Go tae thee bed for mercy's seck."

"Hid ha hipe, hemma," carolled Chloe merrily, "Ha'm han hae he hemmy."

"Whit's shae sayin'?" asked Mrs Harcus sleepily.

"Shae says id's all right, shae's gaun tae be mairried," her husband informed her.

"Shae's stone med, yin lass," remarked Mrs Harcus.

○ ○ ○ ○ ○ ○

The following forenoon Felix, snatching a few minutes off from the harvest work, went to the Post Office for cigarettes, and on the way back he encountered Desdemona Hourston. He stopped with a welcoming smile, but to his consternation the girl walked straight past him, with a set face and her head averted. He dashed after her and grabbed her by the arm.

"Hey, wett a meenit, lass," he cried. "Whit's the idea, wackin' by me like yin?"

"Let go me erm," snapped Desdemona.

"No till thoo tell me whit's the metter? Is id aboot last night? Weel, thoo sees, a'm aafil sorry aboot id, bit—"

"Thoo dinno need tae explain," said Desdemona icily. "Thoo kin plaze theesel whar thoo go tae. I wetted on thee till near fower o'clock, an' thoo niver cam', an' I gret mesel tae sleep. Likely thoo wur wi' some ither lass. Weel thoo kin cheust hed gaun wi' her."

"No no lass, thoo're ferly wrong," said Felix. "Id's like this. I wur on me wey tae thee hoose right enough, bit id

cam' an aafil thick mist, an' I lost me wey." He debated
with himself whether he should tell her that he had gone to
Chloe Harcus's window by mistake, but decided not to.
Desdemona might not see the funny side of it. Weemin were
queer that way. "So I cheust gied home," he finished
somewhat lamely.

Desdemona looked at him scornfully. "Fine day," she
scoffed. "I lukked oot o' me window aboot a quarter past
twelve, an' I could see plain. Thir wis no mist an' the meun
wur shinin'."

"Desh, thir wis a mist when I wur lukkin' for thee hoose
onywey," said Felix. "I couldno see me hend in front o' me
fiss."

"Whit wur thoo wantin' tae see thee hend for?" asked
Desdemona.

"I wurno wantin' tae see id. That's cheust tae let thee see
hoo thick id wur."

"When time wur this?" asked the girl.

"Cheust comin' aboothands wi' twelve o'clock."

"Id wur clear enough afore quarter past onywey, so thoo
didno wett lang tae see if id wid clear. No doot thoo wur in
a hurry tae git awey tae see this ither lass."

"Thir's no ither lass, a'll tell thee." shouted Felix.
"Thir's cheust thee. Thoo're the only wen I love,
Desdemona. Dis thoo no believe me?"

"No," replied the girl candidly. "If thoo loved me thoo
wid hiv wetted all night for the mist tae go awey, bit thoo
didno even wett quarter o' an 'oor."

Felix chewed his lip in perplexity, wondering how he was
going to get out of this impasse. Perhaps, after all, the best
thing to do would be to tell the truth. He cleared his throat.

"Hid's all right," said Desdemona, who had been
watching him contemptuously, "thoo needs no try tae think
on ony more excuses. An' noo let go me erm, for a'm no
wantin' tae spick more tae thee."

"Cheust thoo wett wen meenit," gritted Felix. "A'm
gaun tae tell thee cheust whit happened. Id wur like—" He
broke off. Chloe Harcus was coming down the road. He
stared at her, with a prickling of the spine, remembering last
night's experience. Chloe certainly looked slightly more

attractive now than she had done in her bedroom, with her face cleansed of greasy ointment and the clamp fixing removed from her nose, but that was about all that could be said. He gave her a brief nod of recognition, but to his surprise, instead of passing by she made straight for him, a beaming smile on her face.

"Hammo Hemip," she greeted him.

"Hallo," said Felix, adding politely, "Hoo er thoo livin'?"

"A'm ham," said Chloe mysteriously, and gave a peculiar titter. She came close to him, and put her arm through his.

Felix stared at her, thunderstruck. He tried to withdraw his arm, but Chloe held it in a vice-like grip. Out of the corner of his eye he saw Desdemona move away a little, with a fixed, stony expression on her face.

"Let me go, Chloe," he muttered in embarrassment. "Whit's wrong wi' thee? Er thoo no weel?"

"A'm hime," said Chloe, and clutched the tighter. She looked up into his face with a coy giggle and added, "Hoom ho hip ahey hae he him a hummy hoo."

Felix groped vainly for the meaning of this gibberish. "I dinno ken whir thoo're sayin'," he replied.

Desdemona spoke. She had been at school with Chloe and can make a rough interpretation of what Chloe says. "I think," she observed frigidly, "shae's sayin' that thoo'll no git awey fae her in a hurry, whitiver shae means be that."

"Whit?" gasped Felix. He looked at Chloe, aghast. "Shae's med," he muttered. "Stone med."

"Ham ho heb," snorted Chloe indignantly. Her expression became coy again, and she elbowed him knowingly in the ribs. "Hem hime har hoo han hae hemmy he, Hemip?"

Desdemona's teeth came together with a click. "Shae's askin' when time thoo're gaun tae mairry her?"

Had it not been for Chloe's grip on his arm, which anchored him firmly to the ground, Felix would have leapt several feet in the air at this startling query.

"Mairry her," he shouted. "Geud goad, the lass min be wanderin' in her mind. I hivno the slightest intention o' mairryin' her."

Desdemona was eyeing him narrowly.

Chloe Harcus came up to the startled Felix Garson and put her arm through his.

"Thir's something funny ahint this," she remarked. "Whit wey shid Chloe come up tae thee an' ask if thoo're gaun tae mairry her?"

"Whit wey indeed?" gasped Felix. "I hivno the fentest idea."

"Hepter hap hipe hoo'll hib hae hemmy he," stated Chloe triumphantly, and Felix, his gaze switching from Chloe to Desdemona, was dismayed to see Desdemona recoil, white to the lips.

"Whit is shae said noo?" he groaned.

"Shae's said all a'm wantin' tae hear," grated Desdemona. "Shae says thoo'll hiv tae mairry her efter last night. So that's whar thoo wur wi', thoo niver comed tae see me. Thoo an' thee mist that thoo lost thee way in indeed. Weel weel, id cheust shaws on that men is all the sam'. Thir all dirts. I kinno say I admire thee tist, bit if thoo prefer Chloe tae me thoo kin hiv her. Bit dinno think thoo kin come craalin' back tae me, for if I see thee comin' up yin ledder tae me room again a'll drap the p— the pocker on thee heid."

Felix tried dazedly to figure out this situation. Somehow Chloe knew he had climbed up to her window last night, but how? Then he remembered that Chloe had been sitting in front of a mirror. She must have seen his reflection. But what game was she up to now? Then he thought he saw it. Blackmail. That was it. She was trying to blackmail him into marrying her. He shook her hand off his arm.

"Wett a meenit, Desdemona," he cried. "I kin explain."

"Explain tae thee Auntie Babbie," snapped Desdemona, turning away. "A'm no wantin' tae hear more o' thee lies. If thoo're ony o' a man at all thoo'll mairry the lass noo, bit for mercy's seck dinno gie me a bid tae the weddeen."

And ignoring Felix's cries for her to come back the girl walked swiftly up the road, fighting back her tears. Felix made to dash after her, but Chloe flung herself on his arm again, and held him back.

Felix turned on her furiously.

"Thoo deshed bizzom," he snarled, "noo luk whit thoo're deun. I suppose thoo saa me fiss in the mirror last night."

Chloe's eyes widened. So Felix knew it too. Boy, this was Fate at work with a vengeance. Quite obviously they were twin souls.

"Weel id wur all a misteck," roared Felix. "I wurno comin' tae thee at all, an' noo thoo're pitten Desdemona wild on me. Mairry thee—geud I widno mairry thee if thoo wur the last lass on the earth, so thoo kin pit yin idea oot o' thee heid."

Chloe shrugged her shoulders and smiled tolerantly. She could have told him it was no use. What was written was written. It would serve no purpose to fight against the stars. She did, in fact, tell him so, but he merely stared at her uncomprehendingly, and replied with rude remarks.

"Ham han home hoo," said Chloe, "hip ha'll hee he hipe." And, patting him affectionately on the arm, she withdrew in the direction of Rumtodly. She was not disturbed by the obvious fact that Felix did not love her at the moment, but, once they were married, love would no doubt come.

The moment Chloe's stocky form was out of sight Felix set off hot foot for Whassigo, bent upon making a clean breast to Desdemona of last night's incident, and throwing himself upon her mercy. It had been a grave error, he now realised, not to have explained the thing to her before Chloe arrived on the scene to complicate matters.

Reaching the farm he galloped swiftly up towards the farmhouse door, but when he was still about six yards distant it was flung open, and a wet, rolled-up dishcloth, vigorously thrown, caught him squarely on the face. He reeled and sat down on the path. Desdemona, arms akimbo, and her whole attitude one of menace and hostility, surveyed him from the doorway.

"Clear fae here," she shot out, "thoo trifler wi' weemin. If thoo're no oot o' sight in wen meenit a'll fling something a deshed sight herder."

"Bit Desdemona," pleaded Felix, "cheust listen tae me."

The girl consulted her wrist-watch, vanished into the lobby, and reappeared, swinging a flat-iron purposefully in her hand.

"Haff a meenit tae go," she stated.

"All right," snapped Felix, preparing to beat a retreat, "a'm gaun, bit thoo'll be sorry. Thoo're all wrong aboot me. Id's a—"

"Quarter o' a meenit," announced Desdemona, and raised the iron to shoulder height.

Felix delayed his departure no longer.

○ ○ ○ ○ ○ ○

The few days that followed were a nightmare for Felix. He quickly discovered that the severance of relations between Desdemona and himself was the least of his troubles, and that in supposing that he could easily rid himself of Chloe's unwelcome attentions he had been grotesquely and horribly off the beam. Chloe adhered to him with a persistence compared to which Sinbad and his Old Man of the Sea were separated by a couple of continents. She called at his house five times a day, and if told that he was not in, parked herself in the kitchen until hunger forced him to show up. She met him coming to and going from work, attached herself to his arm, and prattled blithely and incomprehensibly about their approaching marriage. And always she plied him with the same question: "Hemip, hem hime har hoo han hae hemmy he?" It did no good to repulse her, to tell her that the answer was no and would continue to be no. She always came back, and her complete confidence that the answer would ultimately be yes became frightening. It began to wear Felix down. As the constant drip of water is said to wear away the hardest stone so the persistence of Chloe began to affect Felix. He became nervous and furtive in his manner. Even when he knew himself to be alone, his eyes would dart this way and that in the expectation of seeing Chloe suddenly appear. He would start violently at the least footstep, and if anybody happened to touch him on the shoulder from behind he would bound in the air with a shrill scream. His resistance to Chloe's advances became less violent. He began to accept her company with the hopelessness with which a prisoner accepts his handcuffs. The negative with which he answered

Chloe's inevitable question became toneless and apathetic. He foresaw, with a shrinking dread, that the day could not be far distant when he would crack under the strain, and would answer yes.

One evening he did what he should have done before, and sneaking out of the back window of the farmhouse while Chloe's attention was occupied in the kitchen, he set off for Mucklegutter, to place his problem before old Godfrey Ritch, who is held, in Stenwick, to be an authority on all matters respecting women.

The 87-year-old veteran listened carefully, and sympathetically, to the harrowing story.

"Boy," he vouchsafed at length, "thoo're got theesel in a gey prediceement, an' bes' kens whit wey thoo're gaun tae git oot o'd, for Chloe Harcus is fairfil stickit."

He sucked his pipe thoughtfully for several minutes, and took a long pull at the jug of home brew which is never far away from his elbow.

"Id's diffeecult," he mused, "deshed diffeecult. Tell me boy, is Desdemona Hourston still med on thee for gaun nightin' wi' Chloe?"

"I niver gied nightin' wi' Chloe," snorted Felix. "A'm telt thee whit happened. Dis thoo no believe me?"

"Yaas, yaas, of corse. Bit dis Desdemona ken the rights o'd, an' dis shae believe thee?"

"I dinno ken. Shae widno listen tae me explanation, bit I wrott her a letter efter an' telt her the rights o' the affair, so except shae teur the letter up withoot readin' id shae kens me explanation. Bit that's no whit's worryin' me. No doot I could mak' id up wi' Desdemona all right if I could git clear o' Chloe Harcus. Is id iver happen't tae thee, that thoo wur pestered be a lass an' couldno git clear o' her?"

"Geud yaas," said Godfrey. "Awey back in me young days thir wis a lass whar cam' efter me the sam' as whit Chloe is daein' tae thee."

"An' whit wey did thoo git clear o' her?" demanded Felix, leaning forward eagerly.

"I didno git clear o' her," Godfrey said heavily. "I mairried her. Shae wur me first wife."

Felix relaxed with a weary gesture. It seemed to him that in coming to Godfrey for help he was leaning upon a broken reed.

"A'll go," he grunted. "I see thir's no hopp."

"No no boy, wett a meenit," said the veteran. "Cheust let me think. Tell me this, did Chloe see thee at the window the time thoo gied up the ledder?"

"Weel I didno think id at the time, bit sheurly shae did afore shae kent I wur there. Likely shae saa me fiss in the mirror."

Godfrey laid down his jug of home brew with an exclamation.

"Er thoo sheur?"

"Desh, id's the only wey shae could see me, for her back wur tae me, an' I wur doon the ledder afore shae turned roond."

Godfrey grinned broadly.

"Hid's no laughin'," said Felix resentfully.

"Boy, I see id noo," said Godfrey. "I see the wey Chloe is so sheur thoo're gaun tae mairry her. Cheust tell me this. When time wur id when thoo lukked in an' saa her?"

"Hid wid cheust been aboot the strock o' twelve."

Godfrey nodded as if satisfied.

"That's whit I thowt. Boy, dis thoo ken this, Chloe niver kent thoo wur at her hoose at all that night."

"Thoo're daft," snapped Felix impatiently. "Shae saa me."

"Shae saa thee fiss in the mirror."

"Weel whit's the differ?"

"Thir's a hipp o' differ. Shae saa thee fiss, bit shae didno ken thoo wur aboothands."

Felix rose from his chair with a grunt. Things were bad enough without having to listen to this claptrap from a dottan old feul. "A'm awey," he said, reaching for his cap.

"Sit doon an' listen tae me," said Godfrey. "Whit Chloe wur daein' wur treyin' an ould kepper o' lukkin' in the mirror at midnight—id wur her birthday teu, likely—an' hoppin' tae see the fiss o' her future hussband. A'm hard o' id bein' tried a mony a time. An' cheust at the very meenit that shae lukked in the gless thoo lukked in at the window, an' shae saa thee reflection, an' thowt id wur the supersteetion workin'. So thoo sees, that's the wey Chloe is sheur thoo an' her is gaun tae be mairried. Shae thinks id's all arranged be Fett."

Felix gaped, open-mouthed.

"Geud goad," he gasped. "The deshed gappus."

"Plenty o' weemin is gappuses in yin wey," said Godfrey tolerantly.

Felix considered. It sounded fantastic, but the more he thought of it the more he was convinced that old Ritch had hit the nail on the head. If Chloe believed that supernatural powers were at work to provide her with a husband, that explained the strength of her conviction in her ultimate union with himself.

"Weel, in that case," he burst out excitedly, "all I hiv tae deu is tell Chloe id wur me at the window, an' that me fiss in the gless wurno metchic."

"Yaas," agreed Godfrey, slowly, "bit will shae believe thee? Might shae'll cheust think thoo're sayin' id tae git clear o' her."

Felix's face fell. "Might shae will indeed. Bit whit ither kin I deu?"

Godfrey patted him on the shoulder. "Cheust laeve id all tae me. A'm hin long experience o' handlin' weemin. A'll git thee oot o' this prediceement."

At that moment there was a violent knocking on the door. A voice with which Felix was all too familiar shouted, "Hemip, Hemip. Hum oop."

"Id's Chloe," gasped Felix. "Shae's chissed me her. Whit will I dae?"

"Cheust go wi' her, an' say noathing," Godfrey told him. "Laeve id all tae me."

He opened the door, and Chloe burst in, throwing herself into Felix's reluctant arms. "Hi hard hoob hum here," she cried. "Hib ho hoop hreyin' hae hip ahey hae he. Hum om."

Fixing his arm in an iron grip, she led him outside. Felix turned at the door and gave Godfrey a pathetic look of entreaty. The veteran nodded reassuringly.

As he closed the door behind them Godfrey heard Chloe ask, in a peremptory tone: "Hem hime har hoo han hae hemmy he?" He poured himself out another jug of home brew, resumed his seat beside the fire, and proceeded to think hard.

○ ○ ○ ○ ○ ○

Between Godfrey Ritch and Cuthbert Harcus of Rumtodly relations are not what can be called particularly cordial; thus Harcus was a somewhat surprised, and not greatly delighted man when, a couple of evenings after the events narrated above, the sturdy veteran of Mucklegutter ambled into his farmhouse, and took a seat opposite him by the fireside.

"Yaas," said Godfrey breezily, "id's a grand night noo."

Rumtodly looked at him suspiciously from under his shaggy eyebrows.

"Whit er thoo wantin' here?" he demanded.

"Wantin'," echoed Godfrey. "Lockars a'm wantin' noathing. I wur cheust oot a wack, an' I thowt id wid be fine tae drap in an' see thee, the wey a'm no been in Rumtodly for a lang time."

"No lang enough," replied Harcus bluntly.

"Noo noo, boy," said Godfrey, "id's high time thoo wur forgettan yin ould grievance aboot me keekin' thee oot o' the Plooin' Match Association."

"A'm no forgot id," grunted Rumtodly. "Id wur a dirty trick."

"Desh, id wur theesel tae bleem. Thoo hidno peyed thee subscription for fower 'ear."

"Thoo hidno peyed thee subscription for ten," retorted Harcus, "bit thoo didno keek theesel oot. No, thoo watched hid."

"A'm the presseedent," said Godfrey easily, "an' the presseedent disno pey subscriptions."

"Hid's the first a'm hard o' id," said Harcus sourly.

"Weel, weel," said the veteran, "I didno come here tae reck up all yin ould matters."

"Whit did thoo come here tae reck up?"

"Noathing. Noathing. Cheust a freendly call. Dinno be so ackward, boy. Whar's Chloe the night?"

"Shae's oot."

"Doon at Bursteen, likely, seein' Felix Garson?"

"Likely."

"They tell me her an' Felix is gaun tae be married. Thoo'll be gled o' hid."

For the first time something approaching amiability showed in Harcus's face.

"I am hid feth. Whit he sees in Chloe bitts me, bit geud luck tae him."

"I doot id's whit Chloe sees in him whit coonts," remarked Godfrey. "Or rether, whit Chloe sees in her lookin' gless." He moistened his lips ostentatiously. "Yin wack is made me right drey," he observed.

"Yaas, id's sometimes the wey," agreed Harcus, pointedly settling himself more comfortably in his chair.

Godfrey glanced meaningly at the press. "I could dae fine," he said, "wi' a gless o' home brew."

"No doot," said Harcus.

"Weel, er thoo no gaun tae gie me wen?" demanded Godfrey irritably.

"I hiv neun," said Rumtodly. "Id's all feenished. This hervest wark ferly goes for the home brew."

The veteran of Mucklegutter eyed him narrowly. He was certain that this was a downright lie, but, as he well knew, Harcus of Rumtodly is a difficult man to persuade to part with anything. He tapped the floor with his staff in a resigned manner.

"Weel weel," he said, "little metter. Maybe a'm lucky. They say the Rumtodly home brew is no muckle worth."

Harcus sat up angrily.

"Whar says yin?"

"Oh id's a weel-known fact in the pairish. A'm hard a mony a time that id's no fit tae drink."

"Hid's a lie," roared his host. He rose from his chair. "Wett. Might thir'll be a bottle left, an' thoo kin trey id." He went to the press, and returned with a bottle, which he poured out. "Here," he snorted, "set thee mooth tae yin chug an' tell me whit id's like."

Godfrey carefully suppressed his grin of triumph as he immersed his whiskers in the ale. He took a deep, satisfying draught.

"Geud," he exclaimed, "id's no bed. A'm been daein' thee home brew an inchusteece, boy."

"A'm gled thoo ken id," grunted Harcus.

Godfrey sipped the ale slowly and luxuriously, and talked cheerfully of this and that. At length what he had been waiting for happened. Chloe came in. Her cheeks were flushed, and her cross eyes sparkled with what the veteran, a connoisseur in such things, recognised as the lovelight.

"Weel, lass," he greeted her, "er thoo fixed the dett for thee weddeen yet?"

"Ho hep," said Chloe merrily, "hik hip'm ho he ham hoo."

"That's grand," said Godfrey. He appeared to reflect. "Or maybe id's no."

"Whit dis thoo mean, maybe id's no?" demanded Harcus sharply.

Godfrey turned to Chloe. "A'm hard id said that thoo fixed on Felix for thee husband the wey thoo saa his fiss in the lookin' gless at midnight on thee birthday."

"Hap ho," agreed Chloe.

"Boy boy," muttered Godfrey, and shook his head gravely. "Yin's an aafil unlucky supersteetion."

Chloe looked disconcerted. "Hip hey hap?"

The old man took another sip of his home brew. "Maybe I shidno tell thee," he said.

"No tell her whit?" burst out Harcus. "Whit er thoo drivin' at, Godfrey Ritch?"

"Weel," proceeded Godfrey, as if reluctantly, "a'm hard o' lasses treyin' this kepper a mony a time when they wanted tae find oot whar they wur gaun tae mairry."

"An' did id work?" asked Harcus.

"Oh yaas, id worked all right. They all mairried the fella whar's fiss they saa."

"Weel whit—?"

"Wett a meenit." Godfrey raised a portentous nand. "In every case—every case, mind on—the hussband keeked the bucket no a week efter the mairriage."

Chloe emitted a stifled scream, while her father gasped, "Geud goad, whit wey that?"

Godfrey shrugged. "Whar kens? Id cheust happened. Might id wid happen tae Felix Garson. Thoo widno like tae wacken a day or so efter thee weddeen, lass, an' find a corpse aside thee in the bed?"

"Hip a howp," cried the ashen-faced girl. "Hik hip him I hae?"

"Thir's a fer better supersteetion," proceeded Godfrey, "an' a seffer wen. An' hid's for a lass tae luk in a well o' watter. Shae draps some money in the well, a'll tell thee, an' as seun as the water is caamed doon shae sees the fiss o' her future hussband in id. As a metter o' fact thir's a peedie well right ahint me fermhoose whit's affen been yeused for this."

"A well ahint thee hoose," ejaculated Harcus. "A'm niver hard o' hid afore."

Godfrey raised his jug of ale to hide a smile. Seeing that he had only dug the well that morning this was not altogether surprising.

"Oh yaas, id's been there for lang," he said. "Id's whar me dowter saa the fiss o' the man whar shae mairried."

"He's deid," said Harcus significantly.

"No for thirty 'ear efter he mairried though. Thir's cheust wen thing. This min be deun on the 24th o' the month, or id's no yeuse."

"The morn's the 24th," remarked Harcus.

"Lockars so id iss," said Godfrey, with a realistic start of surprise. "Weel, whit aboot id, Chloe? Wid thoo like tae trey id?"

Chloe shifted indecisively from one foot to the other.

"Hik hip hif hip ho Hemip?" she demurred.

"Id might be Felix's fiss that thoo'll see," said Godfrey. "If id iss that means that thoo're seff in mairryin' him."

"An' hib hid ho?"

"Weel if id's no id kinno be helped," cut in Rumtodly brusquely. "Thoo'll cheust mairry whariver's fiss id iss that thoo see."

"Hip hi hipe Hemip," wailed Chloe.

"Desh Felix," snapped her father. "Id's better tae be mairried tae a fella whar thoo dinno like than tae a corpse whar thoo dis like. Thoo'll go an' luk doon in this well the morn."

Chloe considered. There was a good deal of sense in what her father said. A dead man, however good-looking, would be a poor bedmate. It would be a pity if a new face should appear to her in the pool just as she had got Felix nicely softened up for marriage, but still, life was full of these irritations.

"Hang ho," she decided.

Godfrey rose with an air of satisfaction, finished his home brew and picked up his staff.

"Geud for thee, lass. Come ower at aboot three o'clock. An' dinna forget thee money tae fling in the watter. Haff a croon wid be the best. In fact, thoo'll better tak' wen or two haff-croons, for the fiss disno always shaw at the first time."

Bidding the master of Rumtodly and his daughter a cordial goodnight he left the farm and set off at a brisk pace for Mucklegutter. So far, so good, he reflected.

o o o o o o

At a little after half past two the following afternoon Godfrey stood at the gate of Mucklegutter, glancing reflectively up and down the road. All was just about ready for Chloe. He had just poured a couple of buckets of water into his little wishing well. All that remained was to find someone whose reflection Chloe could see in the water, and he did not anticipate any difficulty about that. His only anxiety was in case Chloe should change her mind, and not come. Weemin, as he had often found occasion to notice in his long lifetime, were queer and unpredictable creatures, and Chloe might at the last moment decide that a bird in the looking glass was worth two in the wishing well, and that even should Felix fail to survive the marriage ceremony for more than a few days it was better to be a widow who had tasted the joys of the nuptial embrace than a spinster who had not.

Up the road, cycling slowly, in the manner of one who has plenty of time on his hands, came Armstrong Tait, and Godfrey nodded approvingly. A victim had been delivered into his hands. Armstrong, a bachelor of not unpleasing appearance, and about thirty summers, filled the bill to perfection.

He stepped into the road and gestured, and Armstrong dismounted, and said genially, "Weel, Maister Ritch, whit is id?"

"Cheust come in the hoose a meenit, boy," said the veteran. "I hiv an ould photta o' thee grandfether whit I cam across, an' I thowt thoo wid maybe like tae see id."

"Weel a'm no aafil parteeclar," replied Armstrong. "I hiv aboot a dizzen phottas o' the ould geup mesel."

"An' thoo kin tak' a gless o' home brew in the time thoo're lukkin' at id," added Godfrey quickly.

"That's different," said Armstrong, and he followed the old man into the house with alacrity. Godfrey led him to a small room at the rear of the farmhouse, gave him a chair by the window, poured him out a glass of ale, and thrust a musty velvet-covered album into his hands, with the words: "Id's some wey in there. Cheust tak' a luk an' see if thoo kin find id, an' a'll cheust be back."

Leaving Armstrong sipping home brew and uninterestedly glancing at old and faded photographs he hurried out to the road again. In a little over five minutes he sighed with relief to see Chloe approaching, her short, bandy legs twinkling with her haste.

"Weel, lass," he greeted her, "thoo're got here."

"Harf he hem?" asked Chloe, wasting no time in unnecessary chatter. Her eyes were gleaming with suppressed excitement.

"Hid's cheust ahint the hoose," said Godfrey. "Noo, listen tae me, an' mak' sheur thoo ken whit tae deu. Go roond tae the well, an' stend wi' thee back tae the wall o' the hoose, an' bend doon, an' drap thee haff-croon in, an' in the time the watter is ripplin' say tae theesel, 'I wish tae see the fiss o' me future hussband.' An' as seun as the watter caams thoo shid see id. Er thoo got that?"

Chloe nodded.

"Thoo're no forgot thee money, I hopp?"

"Ham ho hib," said Chloe, opening one hand to display four glittering half-crowns.

"That's grand," said Godfrey. "If thoo dinno see the fiss the first time cheust keep treyin'. Go on noo, lass, an' geud luck. A'll go in the hoose the wey thoo'll no be interupted."

Watching Chloe go round the corner of the house he quickly rejoined Armstrong, who was still turning over pages of the album with an expression of intense boredom.

"Weel, er thoo seen him yet?" asked Godfrey.

"Not I," replied Armstrong. "Boy whit queer-like rigoots they wore in them days. Id's—" He broke off, listening, and said, "Thir's somebody ootside."

"S-sh," whispered Godfrey. "Id's Chloe Harcus. I saa her gaun roond. I winder whit shae wants. No, dinno luk yet. Cheust listen."

They heard the creak of stays as Chloe bent down, then a tiny splash, a mutter of words, a lengthy silence, and a dissatisfied grunt.

Armstrong, overpowered by curiosity, moved to look out of the window, but Godfrey motioned him urgently back. They listened again. Once again came the tiny splash, the mutter, the silence, and then a somewhat more emphatic grunt. A third time this sequence of events occurred, only this time the grunt at the end was replaced by a pronounced snort of vexation. Godfrey waited anxiously. Had he overplayed his hand? No. For the fourth time they heard the little splash, followed by the mutter.

He gave Armstrong a quick nudge. "Luk oot noo, an' see whit shae's daein'."

Tait popped his head out of the window, and looked down. Chloe was immediately underneath him, kneeling down, and peering intently into a hole full of muddy-looking water. Then Godfrey jerked him back into the room.

From outside they heard an exclamation.

"Hamhom Hepp." Then, more loudly and thoughtfully, "Hamhom Hepp."

Godfrey knew what Chloe was thinking. She was comparing her new destiny with her old, and reflecting that while it might have been better there was no doubt but what it could have been worse.

There followed the scrape of feet on gravel, and the sound of swiftly retreating footsteps. Glancing out of the window Godfrey saw Chloe disappearing round the corner of the house.

"Whit on earth wur shae deuin'?" asked the mystified Armstrong Tait, "Kneelin' there, lukkin' in a hole o' watter. Geud secks, a'm affen thowt yin lass wurno ferly witty, an' noo a'm sheur o' id. An' whit wur yin shae wur sayin'? Id soonded like 'Hamhom Hepp'."

"Thoo'll maybe find oot yet," said Godfrey dryly. He gave Armstrong an amused glance. "Wid thoo like tae mairry Chloe?"

Armstrong started violently. "Me mairry Chloe?" He roared with laughter. "Boy, that's a geud wen. Thoo're me dido, Godfrey. Weel, a'll awey. A'm no seen thee photta o' me grandfether, bit id disno metter."

From an upstairs window Godfrey watched him cycle off. He had gone perhaps two hundred yards when a stocky figure darted out into the middle of the road and barred his progress.

"He'll seun ken whit Hamhom Hepp means noo," the veteran sardonically remarked to himself. He poured himself a jug of home brew, donned his hat, and set off for Burstin to inform Felix Garson that the blight had been removed from his life, and transferred to that of Armstrong Tait.

But first he went round to the back of the farmhouse and scooped four half-crowns out of the wishing well. It occurred to him that this could be turned into a highly profitable racket.

The Poison Pen

It was a miserable November evening. Rain, driven by a gusty wind, sheeted down through the darkness, and battered on the bent head and shoulders of the solitary pedestrian who was splashing through many puddles towards the Post Office.

It was impossible to tell whether the figure was a man or a woman. It wore a sou'wester, a long, voluminous oilskin coat, and rubber boots. Reaching the Post Office door it dealt the woodwork a series of vigorous thumps, bent down and pushed something under the door, and then scuttled smartly round the corner of the house.

○ ○ ○ ○ ○ ○

In the dwelling-house which forms the rear part of the Post Office, Geordie Manson the blacksmith, his wife Janet, the postmistress of Stenwick, and the twins, George and Cleopatra, were enjoying a quiet, domestic evening. Geordie was reading, or trying to read, the *People's Journal;* Janet was darning a sock; Cleopatra was climbing up the back of her father's chair in a thrice-frustrated effort to reach the mantelpiece, where there was a china vase upon which she had long cast a covetous eye; George, in something of a tantrum at his repeated failure to strangle the kitten, was hurling his clockwork train at a portrait of his late grandfather for which, ever since he could walk, he has had an inordinate dislike.

Mrs Manson cocked an eye at Cleopatra, who was now standing precariously balanced on the top of the armchair.

"Yin bern's gaun tae fall," she observed. She proved a true prophet. With an ear-splitting scream Cleopatra crashed into the fireplace. Geordie flung down his paper, and leapt to her aid. Moving, as he did so, into his son's line of fire, he stopped the clockwork train with his left ear. Cleopatra's shrieks and Geordie's howl of pain blended with George's howl of annoyance at this interception of what had looked like a throw bang on the target. Rushing at his father, he kicked him on the shin with a violence remarkable in one of his tender years, and then, picking up his train, slung it petulantly at Cleopatra.

Mrs Manson regarded this little fracas with the detachment of one who had seen it happen many a time before, but as her husband, having plucked Cleopatra from the fireplace, was about to take a swing at George with the flat of his hand she broke in sharply: "Dinno hit the bern. If thoo hid been watchin' the peedie lass instead of readin' yin dirt o' pippers it widno hiv happened."

"I dinno see thee watchin' her muckle theesel," snarled Geordie.

"I watch them plenty when thoo're oot at thee wark," retorted his wife. "Noo stoop, an' go an' see whar's at the door. I hard somebody knockin' a meenit ago."

"Go theesel," retorted Geordie. "Id's thee shop. Id'll likely be some geup for fegs."

"I get deshed little help fae thee," said his wife scathingly. "Thoo'll no luk efter the berns, an' thoo'll no dae wen thing. Id's a peety I iver mairried thee."

"Thoo mairried me?" Geordie sneered. "That's geud. Thoo chissed me till I wur forced tae tak' thee. Boy boy, I wur a feul right enough."

Tight-lipped, Mrs Manson got up and went through to the front shop, and unbolted the door. There was nobody outside. She looked up and down the rainswept road in some surprise. There was not a soul in sight. She shrugged her shoulders. No doubt whoever it was had got tired of waiting. She shut the door and was about to withdraw again to the warmth of the kitchen when she noticed an envelope lying just inside the door. She picked it up, noting that it was addressed simply "Janet Manson." Inside was a half sheet of notepaper, on which was printed, "Watch thee man. He's aafil freendly wi' Delilah Bews. She comes tae his smiddy every day, an' steys a while.—A Freend."

The postmistress stared at this missive with an ashen face. Not for an instant did she think of doubting it. Like most wives she had little faith in her husband's fidelity, believing that he was to be trusted only as far as she could see him. Delilah Bews, eh? Yin brazen bizzom. So that was why, of late, Geordie had shown such eagerness to get out of the house and off to his work. Weel, weel. He had kept his intrigue pretty dark, but the truth was out now.

With a set face she returned to the kitchen. Geordie was sitting with Cleopatra on his knee, comforting her with a piece of toffee. George was absorbedly scratching on the sideboard with one of his mother's knitting needles.

"Weel," asked George, "whar wis id?"

"Not a body," said the postmistress. She sat down, folded her arms and regarded him through narrowed eyes, without speaking, for some minutes.

"Whit er thoo geppin' at me for?" he demanded irritably.

"Cheust winderin'," said his wife, "whit Delilah Bews kin see in thee."

Geordie looked puzzled.

"Whar?"

"Delilah Bews. I ken all aboot id."

"All aboot whit? Whit's all this aboot Delilah Bews?"

Janet unclenched her hand, and tossed him the letter. He read it with popping eyes.

"I suppose," said Mrs Manson, "thoo'll tell me id's a lie."

"Of coorse id's a lie," roared Geordie. "Nobody bit a geup like thee wid believe an anoneemous letter like this. A freend, eh? Some freend. Thir always carefil no tae sign thir neem, I notteece. If I kent whar wrott this I wid keek him fae here tae Dounby."

"Thir's no smock withoot fire," said Mrs Manson.

"Whar's spickan aboot smock," snorted her husband. "Dinno change the subchect. Whar gied thee this letter?"

"Id wur leyin' in the door."

"I thowt id. Cheust some sneck in the gress treyin' tae mak' trouble atween iss."

"Is Delilah Bews iver been in thee smiddy?"

Geordie flushed a little.

"Weel, shae wur in a week ago. Shae brock the pedal o' her bike an' wur wantin' me tae trim id."

"Noo wur hearin' aboot id, though," said Janet. "This is the first a'm hard aboot this."

"Geud goad," shouted Geordie, "id wur noathing."

"Is shae been in again?"

"Shae wur in the day efter, for the pedal still wurno right, so I trimmed id again."

"Id says in the letter that shae's been gaun in every day, an' steyin' a while."

"Id's a lie," gritted Geordie. "Id's a dirty lie."

"Thoo're in an aafil stit if id's a lie. A'm notteeced thoo're in a gey hurry tae get awey tae thee wark this peedie while. No doot id'll be tae cairry on wi' Delilah Bews in the smiddy."

"Noathing o' the kind. If thoo want tae ken I cheust go oot o' the hoose the wey I kinno get paece tae tak' me maet for the berns. An' onywey a'm busy."

"So thoo say."

"My mighty, dis thoo no believe me?"

"Not I. Thoo always hid a fancy for ither lasses."

"Bit no fae I mairried."

"No as fer as I ken, bit I dinno ken all whit goes on in the smiddy."

Geordie got up with a scowling face.

"A'm awey tae me bed," he announced. "The morn a'll tak' yin letter tae Timothy Curseeter the bobby, an' wae'll seun find oot whar this whalp is whar's gaun aroond spreadin' lies aboot me."

o o o o o o

Just about the time that Geordie was angrily stamping upstairs to his bed, Tristram Mainland of Drydivot was standing, with a grim face, reading a letter he had picked up in the farmhouse lobby. It said: "Veronica o' Quoydunt is no as faithful as thoo think. When shae's no meetin' thee shae's meetin' Lancelot Hourston.—A Freend."

Though he had been unofficially engaged to the beautiful Quoydunt landgirl for some time, Tristram was well aware that Veronica had many admirers, none of whom made any secret of their wish to supplant himself in her affections. Of these admirers one of the most persistent was Lancelot Hourston, the somewhat dandified son of Silas Hourston of Whassigo. If Tristram has a fault it is that he has a somewhat jealous and suspicious nature, and thus, although his first impulse was to fling the anonymous letter contemptuously in the fire, he did not do so, but sat reading it over and over again, with suspicion gnawing more and more deeply into his brain. Perhaps even now, he reflected, Veronica was over at Whassigo. Why should anyone go to the trouble of writing this letter and delivering it personally on a night like this if there was not some truth in it?

Suddenly he went to the telephone and rang up Quoydunt. The call was answered by Mrs Clouston.

"This is Tristram Mainland spickan," said the young farmer. "Will thoo tell Veronica I want tae spick tae her?"

"Bit Veronica's no in," came the reply.

Tristram's mouth closed like a trap. He opened it again to ask: "Whar is shae?"

"Bes' kens," replied Mrs Clouston. "Shae cheust gied oot, an' niver said whar shae wis gaun. Will I tell her tae ring thee up when shae comes in?"

"Niver mind," said Tristram curtly, and hung up. For several minutes he stood glaring at the phone with glittering eyes. So—she was out, was she? It looked as if "A Freend" was not far wrong. He reached for the phone again and rang Whassigo.

"Hallo," answered the fruity voice of Silas Hourston. "Whar's yin?"

"Is Veronica o' Quoydunt there?" grated Tristram.

"Veronica? Oh yaas, shae's ben in the room wi' me son Lancelot. Cheust a meenit."

There was a short silence, and then, with a pang, Tristram heard his sweetheart's voice. "Hullo. This is Veronica. Who's speaking?"

Tristram dropped the phone into the bracket with a crash. He had heard all he wanted to hear. Veronica was

Tristram Mainland stared grimly at the phone. So it was true;
Veronica was at Whassigo with Lancelot Hourston.

there at Whassigo, with Lancelot Hourston. It was all true.

He stalked back to the kitchen, flung himself into a chair and stared long and bleakly into the fire. The tortoiseshell cat, Sheba, coming to jump into his lap, was surprised and aggrieved to find herself picked up and hurled across the room to the accompaniment of a volley of good round oaths.

"My mercy, Tristram," exclaimed his mother, coming in to see what all the racket was about, "whit's taen thee at the peur cat?"

Tristram rose from his chair, and flung an accusing finger, first at Sheba and then at his mother.

"Niver mention weemin tae me again," he shouted "Thee sex is all the sam'. Thir's no wen thoo kin trust."

○ ○ ○ ○ ○ ○

Four other farmhouses received a visit from the lone figure in the sou'wester and oilskins that night. In each case a letter, signed "A Freend", was left, either poked under the door, or flung into the lobby. Each letter was short and to the point. Eustace Rosie of Spoot-ebb got one which read: "Thoo maybe think Enoch Craigie kin be trusted as treasurer o' the Community Centre, bit whar did he get the money tae buy his new tractor?" The missive addressed to Drusilla Matches of Quoyraffle ran: "The sooner thoo're feenished wi' Gabriel Stoot the better. He his a notion on Portia Rosie." Niobe Spence of Freck received the following: "Dis thoo ken the wey thoo wurno picked as Miss Stenwick at the Harvest Home dance? Ask Andromeda Laird whar bribed the chudges tae pass thee ower." And the recently married Galahad Davie of Pleeps was thrown into a ferment to find himself the recipient of this bombshell: "Thee wife his anither hussband in Sooth Ronaldshay."

The next day found Stenwick swept with suspicion, distrust and bitterness as with a plague. Eustace Rosie hastily convened a meeting of the Community Centre Committee, to which Enoch Craigie was not invited. Galahad Davie sent his wife into hysterics by accusing her of bigamy. Drusilla Matches called on Gabriel Stout, and after a passionate outburst in which she described him as a chit, a double-crossing whalp, a sneck in the gress, a worthless clurt, and other choice epithets, slung her engagement ring in his face. Niobe Spence went about informing all and sundry of the underhand methods by which Andromeda Laird had got herself elected "Miss Stenwick."

Tristram Mainland, meeting Veronica on the road, passed her with a look of frozen indifference.

"Tristram," she cried, looking after him in consternation, "what's the matter?"

"Noathing," he replied coldly, turning, "noathing at all."

"Are you annoyed because I wasn't in when you phoned last night?"

Tristram shrugged his shoulders. "Id's neun o' me business if thoo're in or oot."

"I was at Whassigo, if you want to know."

Tristram shrugged again. "Thoo kin go whar thoo like, sheurly. Id's a free country."

"I went to see Lancelot Hourston—"

"A gret admirer o' thine."

"— to discuss a show we're putting on for the Community Centre at Christmas."

"No doot," said Tristram politely. "Weel, weel, a'm in a hurry." He turned away and walked on.

"Tristram," cried the landgirl desperately, "you'll be coming up tonight to take me to the pictures?"

But Tristram gave no sign of having heard.

And from the Post Office Geordie Manson left for his work in a chill atmosphere.

"Thoo needno bother tae come home for thee denner," snapped his wife. "Cheust go an' get id fae Delilah Bews."

Having thus sped her husband on his way she went back into the house to ponder over the question of how one set about getting a divorce.

o o o o o o

Geordie did not, in fact, come home for his dinner. Nor did he follow his wife's suggestion and get it from Delilah Bews. At one o'clock he mounted his bicycle with a purposeful air and rode to the cottage which serves as the Stenwick outpost of the Orkney Police Force.

Police Constable Timothy Cursiter was making short work of an appetising lunch of steak and clapshot when the parish blacksmith beat a resounding tattoo on the door and stamped aggressively into the kitchen. Timothy frowned slightly, for he was a man who disliked being interrupted at the serious business of eating.

"Weel boy," he demanded brusquely, "whit's the metter?"

"This is the metter," snapped Geordie, and he flung down the anonymous letter on the table. The constable read it carefully and looked at Geordie with an expression of some censure.

"Boy," he said, "this is an aafil cairry-on for a mairried man."

"Desh thee," snorted Geordie, "id's no true. Id's a pack o' lies. That's the wey a'm taen id tae thee tae investeegett."

The constable elegantly wiped gravy from his mouth with the edge of the tablecloth and subjected the letter to another close scrutiny, back and front. At length he looked up and said, in the tone of one who has made an important discovery: "Hid's anoneemous."

"Of corse id's anoneemous," hooted Geordie. "That's the wey a'm comed wi' id tae thee. If I kent whar wrott it I wid hiv gone an' hemmered the livin' daylights oot o' him."

"Whar dis thoo think wrott id?" asked Timothy.

"Bes' kens," grunted Geordie. "Some whalp whar hetts me guts, onywey."

"Weel, whar all hetts thee guts?"

"I didno think thir wis onybody whar didno like me tae that extent. Might id could be Vernon Isbeester, bit he kinno write."

"Onybody ither?"

Geordie pondered. "Ermstrong Tett isno very freendly wi' me, bit I herdly think he wid write anoneemous letters tae me wife, sayin' I wur gaun wi' Delilah Bews."

"Weel, a'll tell thee," said Timothy, a trifle impatiently, for he was anxious to get on with his dinner, "cheust laeve the letter wi' me, an' a'll mak inquiries."

Geordie took his departure, and Timothy promptly forgot about the matter. It was recalled to his notice, however, about an hour later, when a deputation from the Stenwick Community Centre Committee, headed by Eustace Rosie, called on him and produced an anonymous letter casting doubts on the trustworthiness of Enoch Craigie of Swashmidden, the Committee's treasurer.

"Thoo sees, boy," explained Eustace, "id's maybe true, an' id's maybe no true, bit wae wid like thee tae go an' see Enoch an' mak' sheur he's no been makkin' free o' the funds."

"Why no go an' see him theesels?" inquired Timothy, taking a poor view of the assignment.

"Weel, wae dinno want ony ill-feelin' wi' Enoch," mumbled Eustace Rosie, shifting uncomfortably, and the deputation withdrew.

The constable compared the letter received by Eustace Rosie with that received by Mrs Janet Manson, and discovered, as he had suspected, that they were undoubtedly written by the same person. The notepaper was exactly similar; so was the ink; and the printing, so far as he could judge, was alike. In the light of this, the case, it seemed to him, took on a wider scope. Someone, obviously, had an ill will at Enoch Craigie as well as at Geordie Manson. Later in the afternoon it was brought home to him that the scope of the case was even wider, for he had a visit from Niobe Spence of Freck, with another of the anonymous letters.

Timothy began to get excited. He realised that what he had run up against was a poison pen campaign, the first of his experience. By a happy coincidence he had recently read a crime story by Agatha Christie dealing with this very subject, so that he considered himself thoroughly experienced in this form of slander, and well-equipped to crack this Stenwick case wide open. First he set about finding out whether any other anonymous letters had been received besides the three he already had, and before evening he was in possession of the knowledge that letters had also been received by Drusilla Matches and Galahad Davie, from which it was only a short step to being in possession of the actual letters.

The next stage was to ascertain what truth, if any, lay in the allegations or innuendoes which the letters contained, and this part of the investigation did not enhance Timothy's popularity. The first reaction of Enoch Craigie, when questioned as to whether he had been misusing the Community Centre funds, was to attack the constable with a creepie, but after Timothy had successfully dodged the assault for ten minutes the master of Swashmidden calmed down, and with an ill grace consented to an examination of his Community Centre cash box and books. Satisfied that Craigie was on the square, and that the poison pen had been wide of the mark in this case, Timothy went on to Pleeps, where he had an even more hostile reception from Mrs Galahad Davie, Galahad not being present, as he had gone to stay with his parents. Mrs Galahad passionately declared that she was no bigeemist and no crimeenal, and that the letter sent to her husband had been a foul slander, and that she could easily have satisfied Galahad on that point if he had waited long enough to listen. Furthermore, she declared, she did not want the police boring into her affairs, and that unless Timothy took himself off she would set about him with a red-hot poker. Timothy withdrew hastily, consoling himself with the reflection that he could get the South Ronaldsay police to check up on Mrs Galahad's past history. (He did so, in fact, later, and discovered that while Galahad's wife's record was not free from blemish, she had never actually been married to another man.)

Andromeda Laird, when closely questioned about the letter sent to Niobe Spence, hotly denied that there had been any hanky-panky about her election as "Miss Stenwick." It was, she stated, all "soor grepps" on Niobe's part, and Timothy could, if he wanted, get confirmation from the panel which had judged "Miss Stenwick." The constable did question the panel, consisting of Messrs Judas Corrigall, Titus Sinclair, and Ananias Kelday, and while privately convinced that he had never seen a trio more likely to stoop to chukery-packery, he could not shake their statements that the election of "Miss Stenwick" had been entirely above-board.

As for the Drusilla Matches-Gabriel Stout business, a sullen Gabriel told the constable that Drusilla had been making a fuss about nothing, and that while it was true that under the influence of home brew he had given Portia Rosie a jocular slerp in a dark corner at a recent dance, he could by no means be described as having a notion of her.

It was a slightly depressed Timothy who returned home after these investigations, and settled down with his notebook and a glass of home brew to think things over. His first confidence that he would be able to crack this case open with no bother had withered considerably, and indeed, as he sipped his home brew, he toyed with the thought of throwing in his hand and turning the case over to headquarters in Kirkwall, who would be able to put a qualified detective on the job. On reflection, however, he cast this defeatist idea aside, for the time being at any rate, for if he could unmask the poison pen single-handed a sergeant's chevrons might be his reward.

Sighing, he buckled to the task of sorting out what he had already unearthed. The allegation regarding Enoch Craigie was clearly unfounded. Mrs Galahad Davie was not a bigamist, but she had a murky past. Andromeda Laird might, or might not, have been elected "Miss Stenwick" on false pretences. As far as the allegations against Geordie Manson and Gabriel Stout were concerned they appeared to be based on isolated incidents, magnified out of all proportion.

It occurred to him that the author of the anonymous letters knew a good deal that it was none of his, or her, business to know, and was in close touch with parish gossip and scandal. Who could it be?

And at this point Timothy sat up with so violent a jerk that he knocked his glass of ale off the arm of the chair. There was one person who had all the qualifications necessary to be regarded as his leading suspect. Mrs Janet Manson, the postmistress. She was the outstanding busybody in the parish, and what she did not know about the private lives of Stenwick's population was not worth knowing. What she did know was not worth knowing either, if it came to that, but it would certainly provide excellent material for anonymous letters.

Timothy was not disturbed by the fact that Mrs Manson herself had received one of the poison letters. From his crime reading he knew that that was one of the oldest of gags. What better way to divert suspicion than to write an anonymous letter to herself? It was a blind, a bluff, but he, Timothy Cursiter, had seen through it.

Blithely he leapt from his chair, and poured himself another glass of home brew. Yes, he had cracked the case wide open.

o o o o o o

The following forenoon Timothy entered Geordie Manson's smiddy with a somewhat wary step. Geordie was busy, but he was not happy at his work like the village blacksmith immortalised by Longfellow. A black scowl rested on Geordie's brow and he was battering at a tractor axle which rested on his anvil with a violence beyond what was necessary. Indeed it was as well the owner of the axle was not present.

"Ay boy," said Timothy.

Geordie glanced up. His scowl did not lift, but he grunted. "Weel, er thoo fand oot onything?"

The constable prudently positioned himself so that the anvil was between Gerdie and himself.

"I hivno got defeenite proof yet," he replied, "bit I hiv a strong suspeecion whar the guilty pairty is."

Geordie's eyes gleamed. His mighty shoulders squared, and his muscles knotted as he tightened his grasp of his hammer.

"Whar is id?" he demanded. "Tell me an' a'll go right fae here an' drive his heid doon intae his body."

"Id's no a him," said the policeman. "Id's a her."

Geordie looked surprised, as if this possibility had not occurred to him before.

"Weel, whar is shae?" he grated.

"Tae tell the truth, Cheordie," said Timothy, "I suspect thee wife."

Geordie's hammer dropped from his hands, and hit him on the toe. When he finished dancing with pain he hobbled towards the constable, his hands spasmodically clenching and unclenching. Timothy backed away.

"Tak' id aisy, boy," he muttered.

"Tak' id aisy," roared the smith. "Thoo gret clurt. Thoo gappus. Dis thoo mean tae say thoo suspect Chenet o' bein' this anoneemous writer? My mighty boy, shae got a letter hersel."

"I ken hid," replied Timothy, "bit hid wis maybe cheust a bluff."

"Dinno be a geup. I wis there when shae got id. Shae hard a knock at the door, an' gied tae answer id, an' the letter wur leyin' in the lobby."

"Did thoo hear the knock?"

"Not I. The berns wis keekin' up ower muckle noise."

"Cheust so. Did thoo see Chenet pickin' up the letter?"

"Whit wey could I see her? I wur in the kitcheen."

"So as fer as thoo wur concerned thir wis no knock, an' shae could cheust as weel hiv hin the letter in her pocket afore she iver gied tae the door."

Geordie's eyes widened. "Geud goad," he gasped. "Id kinno be— No. Wait a meenit. Chenet wur ferly stunned when shae read the letter. She cam' back tae the kitcheen ferly barmin' an' gied me an aafil time. Shae widno hiv cairried on like yin if id wir her whar wrott the letter."

"Cheust a pit-on," said Timothy, shrugging his shoulders.

Geordie's expression changed again. He looked like someone who had just discovered that he was nourishing a viper in his bosom.

"My mighty," he growled. "The deshed bizzom indeed. Bit wett ye, wett ye. A'm gaun right home tae tell her whit I—" With his jacket half on he froze, and then turned to the policeman with a shout.

"Whit aboot this ither letters? Chenet couldno hiv hid noathing tae deu wi' them, so thoo're ferly wrong aboot her. Shae wurno over the door that night."

Timothy's face fell. "Er thoo sheur?" he asked.

Geordie considered. "No, desh, a'm no sheur," he muttered. "Thoo sees, efter me an' Chenet hid wur row I gied tae me bed, an' I dinno ken when time Chenet cam', for I wur soond asleep, an' niver hard her comin' in the bed."

"So shae could hiv been oot, an' delivered this ither letters?"

Geordie passed a hand dazedly across his brow. "Hid's posseeble," he reluctantly admitted.

Timothy smiled grimly. The net was closing around Mrs Janet Manson.

"Tell me boy," he inquired, "when time wur id that Chenet got this letter?"

Geordie considered. "Hid wid be a piece efter nine. Aboot haff past."

"Well, a'll check up wi' the ithers whar got letters when time they got them, an' efter that I doot a'll hiv tae come roond an' charge thee wife, boy."

But, alas for Timothy, when he came to check up on the time of receipt of the other letters he found his case against the postmistress blown sky-high. Eustace Rosie had received his letter at some time between 8.30 and nine, and Niobe Spence had got hers lying in the lobby at 9.15. And there was indisputable proof that Janet Manson had not left her house before half past nine.

Overcoming his disappointment, the constable looked about him for the next most promising suspect, and decided that Enoch Craigie was a possibility. Might it not be the case that Enoch had sent Eustace Rosie that accusation against himself as a red herring, well knowing that he could easily disprove it. Timothy could conceive of no reason why Enoch should spread lies and calumnies, for though an irascible type, Enoch had never been regarded as a scandalmonger; nevertheless he investigated this line of thought, and discovered that Craigie had a perfect alibi, having been at home in the company of Godfrey Ritch of Mucklegutter from half past seven to half past ten. Timothy felt some relief at being able to put Enoch in the clear, as he was affianced to Enoch's daughter, and it would have been unpleasant to have a poison pen for a father-in-law.

In his inquiries into the alibis of Galahad and Mrs Davie, Niobe Spence and Drusilla Matches he came up against a blank wall. None of them could have been the writer of the anonymous letters. The affair began to get Timothy down.

It was two days later, and still Timothy was no nearer solving the mystery. Three more poison letters had come to light, one declaring that Aeneas Eunson of Nethergeup had forged his uncle's will, under which he had inherited a farm and a nice little nest egg of £5000, the second being directed at Cupid Shearer of Gappusha', accusing him of falsifying his claim for an oat crop subsidy, and the third alleging that Anastasia Groundwater was having an occasional clandestine rendezvous with a gentleman other than her fiance, Jasper Jolly.

Timothy had got to the stage when he was almost tearing his hair. His mother viewed him with some concern as he stamped up and down the kitchen of the cottage, wild-eyed and dishevelled, over and over again demanding of the spirits of the air, "Whar kin id be?"

"Er thoo treyed a process o' elimeenation?" Mrs Cursiter asked. "Id's affen a geud wey tae find oot whar, an' whar no tae suspect."

"Elimeenation," shouted Timothy wildly. "My mighty, mither, a'm treyed hid." He produced three foolscap sheets from his tunic pocket, covered with ticked-off names, and waved them in front of her nose.

"Luk. A'm elimeenated ivery livin' sowl in the parish. Thir's forteen fock whar I thowt might hiv deun id, an' thir all got perfect aleebis. Noo whar dae I go fae here?"

"Might id's somebody no in Stenwick at all," observed Mrs Cursiter.

Timothy flung himself into a chair with a hollow groan. Heaven forbid that he should have to start eliminating the populations of Harray, Stenness, Sandwick, Birsay and Evie. That would be too much.

"No no," he said. "Id min be somebody in Stenwick. Somebody whar I wid niver think tae suspect. Bit whar."

"The mineester, maybe."

Timothy looked shocked.

"My lockars, mither, thoo're no serious?"

"Weel," said Mrs Cursiter, "he's wen that thoo wid niver suspect. A'll no say I think id's him though."

"Whit's the mottive ahint id?" muttered the constable. "Is id somebody cheust oot tae mak' trouble, or is id somebody wi' a defeenite purpose whar is cheust writin' a lot o' ither letters tae compleecate metters?"

"I think id's a wife mesel," said Mrs Cursiter. "Id's the kind o' thing weemin wid dae rither than men."

"I widno say bit thoo're right," agreed Timothy, "bit that disno get me ony nearer findin' oot whar shae is."

"Why no set a trap?" suggested his mother.

"Whit dis thoo mean? A trap. A rebbit trap, dis thoo mean, whit shae wid pit her feet in? Weel, that might dae, bit whar wid I set id, an' whit wey wid I ken I hid catched the right body?'

Mrs Cursiter sighed, reflecting not for the first time that rapidity on the uptake was not her son's strong suit.

"No, thoo geup. No a rebbit trap. Arrange wi' some-body tae go oot an' dae something he shidno be daein'—gaun wi' anither man's wife, maybe—an' might wur freend whar writes the anoneemous letters will rise tae the bett, an' write anither wen, an' thoo kin watch for her deliverin' id."

This took some time to sink into Timothy's grey matter, but when it had done so he bounded from his chair with a yell of admiration.

"My mercy, mither, thoo're hit the nell right on the heid. Yin's a winderfil idea. A'll dae id." He sat down again thoughtfully. "Bit whar will I get tae go wi' somebody else's wife?"

"The less ither fock kens aboot the trap the better," pointed out his mother shrewdly. "Dae id theesel."

"Bit I hivno a wife," demurred Timothy.

"Desh thee for a blockit," snapped his mother impatiently. "Thoo his a sweethert, his thoo no? Aadrey Craigie o' Swashmidden."

Timothy felt his enthusiasm for the idea ebb somewhat.

"Geud," he mumbled, "Aadrey widno like the notion o' me gaun wi' ither weemin. Shae wid tak' ill wi' id."

"Whit a nonsense," scoffed Mrs Cursiter. "Thoo could tell her all aboot id efter thoo're catched the poison pen reid-hended, an' shae wid be prood o' thee."

"A'll dae id," said Timothy with decision, and as he spoke he knew the very girl he would make use of for his purpose, Andromeda Laird. He had long been a secret admirer of Andromeda, a sultry-eyed brunette, of buxom build. Whether or not Niobe Spence had been right in supposing that Andromeda had got herself elected Miss Stenwick by unfair means there was no denying that she ran Niobe close as the parish pin-up girl. Indeed she was considerably better-looking than Timothy's own fiancee, Audrey Craigie, but whereas Audrey was the daughter of a well-to-do farmer, Andromeda's father was a crofter of humble means. In the ordinary way, therefore, Timothy would not have dared to risk Audrey's wrath by making advances to Andromeda, but now that he had the opportunity of doing so with a clear conscience, and in the line of duty, he jumped at the chance.

○ ○ ○ ○ ○ ○

The following afternoon he called at the croft of Hereward Laird, and found the daughter of the house just about to set off to the Post Office for her messages.

"Ay, Andromeda," he greeted her breezily, "hoo er thoo livin'?"

"Oh a'm fine," she said. "Whit er thoo wantin? Er thoo comed tae ask aboot yin letter whit Niobe Spence got again, for id's no true. I wur elected Miss Stenwick fair an' square, so—"

"No no, lass, I believe thee. In fact, if I hid been wen o' the chudges I wid niver hiv lukked twice at ony o' the ither competeetors. Dis thoo ken this, Andromeda, thir's no a lass in Stenwick whar kin hed a candle tae thee."

"No even Aadrey Craigie?"

"Confeedentially, no even Aadrey," whispered the constable.

"Weel if thoo're no wantin' tae ask me aboot the letter, whit er thoo wantin'?"

"Cheust the pleasure o' thee company," said Timothy, with his most winning smile. "Thoo're ready for oot, I see."

"Yaas, a'm cheust gaun tae the Post Office."

"I suppose thoo'll hiv no obchection if I come wi' thee."

"Come if thoo want," replied Andromeda, and they set

out, Timothy with a complacent grin, Andromeda with an expression of some puzzlement.

A little way along the road Timothy slipped his arm round her waist.

"Thoo're a right nice lass," he observed.

"So a'm been telt," she replied, giving him a sidelong glance from under fluttering eyelashes, which sent the policeman's temperature up about ten degrees. Boldly he drew her tighter towards him and mumbled: "Whit aboot a peedie kess?"

"Oot here on the road?" queried Andromeda. "Boy thoo're no faird. Whit wid Aadrey Craigie say?"

"Shae'll no ken," retorted Timothy.

"Shae wid ken all right. Wae kin be seen fae aboot three fermhooses. Might shae wid git wen o' those anoneemous letters."

"A'll chance id," said Timothy, and sweeping her into his arms he dealt her a resounding, if somewhat clumsy slerp on the mouth. "Boy," he said breathlessly, "yin wur geud. A'm been wantin' tae dae yin for a long time. Whit aboot anither?"

But Andromeda pushed him away, her eyes narrowed and suspicious.

"Whit's thee game, Timothy Cursiter," she demanded. "Thir's something ahint this. Whit er thoo start flirtin' wi' me for all o' a sudden? An' in public teu. Id's cheust as if thoo wanted id tae get tae Aadrey Craigie."

Timothy bit his lip in vexation. Andromeda was evidently a lot smarter on the uptake than he had thought. He decided that he might as well take her into his confidence.

"As a metter o' fact, lass," he said, "thoo're right. That's cheust whit I dae want."

"Bit my mercy, whit for? Er thoo fowt wi' her? Er thoo wantin' tae git clear o' her?"

"No no. I cheust want her tae git an anoneemous letter aboot me. An' when the letter's delivered a'll be wettan tae catch the wen whar dis id."

"Weel weel," said Andromeda musingly, "I always took thee for a gappus, but thoo're smerter than I thowt, a piece.

So that's all thoo're been makkin' up tae me for. Thoo his a right neck, a'll tell thee. I hiv a geud mind tae gie thee a skelp on the lug."

"Desh, a'm enchoyed daein' id all the sam'," said Timothy, with a grin, "so dinno be offended, Andromeda."

"Weel a'm enchoyed id mesel'," said the girl, with a laugh which seemed to Timothy heartier than the occasion warranted. "Thoo'll better pit thee erm roond me waist again, an' no spoil id."

Timothy did so and they walked on.

"Of coorse," said the constable warningly, "thoo'll need tae keep this under thee hat."

"A'll deu hid," she promised. "Tell me boy, is thir been ony more o' this anoneemous letters?"

"Neun. Cheust the eight."

"The nine, thoo mean."

"No, cheust eight. Chenet Manson, Enoch Craigie, Drusilla Matches, Galahad Davie, Niobe Spence, Aeneas Eunson, Cupid Shearer, an' Chasper Cholly."

"An' Tristram Mainland."

"Did he get wen? I niver hard aboot hid."

"So I hard. Id's maybe no true."

"Weel if he did that's nine right enough. That's all so fer, bit," and Timothy smiled thinly, "a'm hoppin thir'll be anither the night."

They walked on, watched by a number of interested eyes from farmhouse windows, and at the Post Office they parted company, Andromeda going in for her messages, and Timothy heading home at a brisk lope. The trap, he felt, had been well baited. Now to spring it, and unmask the poison pen.

o o o o o o

It was a dark night, with heavy rain. Timothy, huddled in as much lee as he could get alongside the farmhouse of Swashmidden, was not enjoying his vigil, but he comforted himself with the reflection that the unpleasant conditions were just such as would suit the poison pen for the delivery of a letter.

He had been waiting since half past seven, and it was now half past nine. Rain battered steadily on his cap and cape, and seeped insidiously down his neck. He was numb with cold, and he doubted whether his nerveless fingers were capable of switching on the torch they held when the moment to do so arrived. Nevertheless he stuck it. The arrival of the poison pen he felt, could not be long delayed now, for eight to ten seemed to have been the time schedule for the delivery of previous letters. He had not informed the inhabitants of Swashmidden of his presence, the better to observe secrecy, but there had been moments when only supreme will-power had restrained him from dashing into the farmhouse for a seat by the fire and a cup of hot tea.

Suddenly he tensed. Somebody was coming up the road to the farmhouse. The splash and slither of footsteps became more distinct. Waiting till they were only four or five yards from the farmhouse door the constable rushed from his hiding place, and with a roar of "A'm got thee," launched himself at the shape he could see by the light of the farmhouse window. The shape emitted a feminine scream, and squirmed free from his grasp. Timothy flung himself at its legs and brought it down, full length, with a crash. Standing over it he switched on his torch, and then his jaw dropped in utter consternation.

"A-A-A-aadrey," he stuttered. For the face looking up at him was that of his fiancee.

Audrey Craigie scrambled to her feet, wiped some of the mud out of her eyes, and gasped for breath.

"Timothy," she shouted, "is that thee? Whit er thoo thinkan on, chumpin at me like yin? Thoo near frightened me oot o' me wits. Er thoo med?"

"A'm—a'm sorry lass," groaned Timothy. "I didno ken id wur thee. I thowt thoo wur in the hoose all the time." A horrible suspicion shot across his brain. "Aadrey, thoo're no—thoo kinno be—"

"I dinno ken whit thoo're yappin' aboot," snapped Audrey, "an I dinno ken whit thoo're skulkin' aboot here for in the weet, bit id's cheust as geud thoo er here, for a'm been ower at Snortquoy fae efter tea, an' Cheanick Budge is telt me all aboot yin cairry-on thoo wur haein' the day wi' yin geud for noathing bissom, Andromeda Laird. Slerpin' an' kissin' on the public road indeed. Thoo shid be asheemed tae come near Swashmidden, an' thoo'll no come near id again, for wur feenished, dis thoo hear?"

"Wett a meenit," said Timothy, relieved to hear that Audrey had an alibi for her movements, "thoo dinno understend."

"I understend ower weel," said Audrey. "Go tae thee Andromeda Laird, thoo double-crossing whalp."

"Id wur a trap," persisted Timothy, "tae trey an' catch this poison pen. A'm been wettin' here fae half past siven, hoppin' thir wid be an anoneemous letter delivered tae thee aboot me an' Andromeda."

Audrey relaxed. She would not have put it past Timothy to make passes at Andromeda Laird, but she had been baffled by his doing so in broad daylight. His explanation rang true. He was only a geup, and not, after all, a double-crossing whalp.

"Thoo're a geup, boy," she told him. "Noo, come in an' hae thee supper afore thoo git thee dith o' cowld."

Timothy almost weakened, but with his foot on the doorstep his resolution triumphed.

"No," he said, "me duty comes first. A'll wett ootside in case the poison pen comes."

"Plaze theesel," replied Audrey coldly. "I hopp thoo enchoy id. A'm gaun in tae get me supper an' go tae me bed."

Feeling rather like the boy who stood on the burning deck whence all but he had fled, Timothy resumed his vigil. The hours passed. The lights in Swashmidden went out, and no anonymous letter-writer, or anybody else, arrived. At midnight, chagrined, soaking, and sneezing violently, Timothy decided to call it a day.

○ ○ ○ ○ ○ ○ ○

Next morning, sitting at the window of his cottage, wrapped in a dressing gown and with his feet immersed in a mustard bath, he saw Tristram Mainland passing by on his bike, and hailed him peremptorily.

"Weel, whit is id?" asked the young farmer, coming to the window.

"Thoo niver telt me thoo got an anonemous letter," Timothy accused him.

Tristram stiffened.

"Whar I git letters fae is me business," he retorted. "Whar telt thee I got wen, onywey?"

"Andromeda Laird happened tae mention id tae me. Whit wur in id?"

"Did Andromeda Laird no tell thee hid?"

"No."

"Weel, thoo're gettan no information fae me."

"If thoo'll no tell me thoo're obstructin' the laa," warned the constable.

"Fiddle de diddle," scoffed Tristram, "a'm sayin' noathing." And jumping on his bicycle he pedalled rapidly off down the road.

Tristram had been on his way to the Post Office, but he did not stop there now. He rode on past it, head down, and feet driving at the pedals until he came to Hereward Laird's croft of Sooricks. Dismounting he thrust his way, without ceremony, into the kitchen. Andromeda was there, plucking a hen, and at sight of him she fell back with a gasp.

"Tristram," she cried.

Tristram glared at her contemptuously.

"So id wur thee," he snapped.

"Whit wur me?"

"Fine dis thoo ken whit I mean. Thoo sent me yin anoneemous letter."

The hen dropped from Andromeda's hands and hit the floor with a dull thud.

"Id's a doonright lie," she muttered.

"Weel, whit wey did thoo ken I got id?"

She dropped her eyes in confusion. "I—I—hard it fae somebody in the passin'."

"Thoo did noathing o' the kind. I telt nobody I got the letter. Nobody, dis thoo hear? If thoo kent, thir's only wen wey thoo could hiv. Thoo sent id theesel."

"Whit wid I send anoneemous letters tae thee for?"

"Tae mak' trouble atween me an' Veronica, no doot. Fae

iver shae cam' tae Stenwick thoo're been chealous o' her, an' thoo're been hoppin' I wid gie her up an' come back tae thee."

"Id's no true," said Andromeda, through white lips.

Tristram moved towards the door. "Wid thoo like me tae go back tae Timothy Cursiter, an' tell him whit I think? Wid thoo like tae be in the coort, charged wi' slender?"

Andromeda suddenly burst into tears. "No no, Tristram, dinno dae that. A'll confess. I did id, tae trey an' git thee back tae me. Bit dinno tell the polis."

Tristram looked at her with a touch of pity. "An' whit aboot all this ither letters thoo wrott? Thoo're caased a hipp o' trouble, a'll tell thee."

"I ken," sobbed Andromeda, "bit yin ither letters wur cheust a lot o' dirt, cheust the wey they widno ken whar tae suspect. I pat wen tae Niobe Spence aboot mesel. Tristram, dinno tell the polis, will thoo no? Dinno tell nobody. A'll niver dae id again, I promeese."

"On wen condeetion," said Tristram. "Write a confession aboot the letter thoo sent me, an' a'll shaw id tae Veronica in confeedence, an' then a'll tear id up. Will thoo dae that?"

"Y-y-yaas," whimpered Andromeda.

Ten minutes later Tristram was hurrying to Quoydunt, the confession in his pocket, to make his peace with Veronica.

○ ○ ○ ○ ○ ○

For five more nights Timothy patrolled the outskirts of Swashmidden. He caught no poison pen, nor did he hear of any more anonymous letters being delivered in the parish. He gave up his investigation to save himself from pneumonia, and disgustedly added the poison pen to his already long list of unsolved Stenwick crimes.

The Kidnapped Outside-left

This is the story of the one and only occasion upon which Stenwick Football Club has won the Orkney Inter-Parish Cup. For many years the team's record in this competition was so dismal that the term "as hoppless as Stenwick" became the recognised criterion when it was desired to pass caustic comment upon a particularly feeble display by any team, and when the annual draw for the Parish Cup was made, the club drawing Stenwick in the first round felt itself justified in going ahead with arrangements for the second round tie.

With the advent of Godfrey Ritch of Mucklegutter as president and manager of the club, Stenwick's fortunes took a turn for the better. He boosted morale by instituting the Ritch Cup, a tournament confined to teams in the West Mainland, and played under a set of rules devised by himself, rules so complex and varying—they were sometimes, in fact, invented on the spur of the moment—that it would have baffled the ingenuity of a Royal Commission to interpret them successfully. Invariably, however, these rules operated to Stenwick's advantage. Add to this the fact that old Godfrey was not above such questionable tactics as bribing referees, administering doped oranges to the opposing team at half-time, and engineering spurious telegrams and phone calls to leave the other side short of key players, and it will be understood why Stenwick has enjoyed a considerable amount of success in the Ritch Cup, reaching the final five times, and winning the trophy twice in successive years.

The Parish Cup, however, is a different kettle of fish. Played under Orkney Football Association auspices with referees of high integrity, it offers little scope for hanky-panky, or chukery-packery, and Stenwick's showing in this contest continued to be pretty miserable, though they had improved to the extent of occasionally scraping through to the second round, and once even to the third.

In the season of which this story tells, the club had excelled all previous performances by reaching the final, and enthusiasm in the parish was at fever heat as the day approached. It is true that in getting to the final Stenwick had been considerably aided by fortune. In the first round they had been drawn against Deerness, a team which would normally have pulverised them. Unfortunately for Deerness, on their way to Stenwick to play the first leg of the tie their bus had collided with a cattle float, and seven of their players had been rendered unfit for play. Quick to cash in on the situation, Godfrey had refused to postpone the match, and Deerness, turning out with a scratch team, mainly composed of supporters, had been beaten 14-3. In the return match, at full strength, they had overwhelmed Stenwick 10-nil, but as a simple arithmetical calculation will show, Stenwick passed into the second round with a lead of one goal on aggregate.

Good luck again favoured Stenwick in the second round, against Shapinsay. A mumps epidemic, breaking out on the island, reduced the Shapinsay team, for both legs of the tie, to a mere shadow of its normal strength. Even so, Stenwick were hard pressed to get through 2-0 at home and 3-2 away.

In the third round the Fates continued to smile on Stenwick. At home, in the first game, they were comfortably beaten 4-0 by Orphir. On the eve of the second game there was a big wedding in Orphir, to which all members of the football team were given a bid as a matter of course. They attended under strict instructions from their management committee to lay off the home brew and the bridescogs, but though the spirit was willing, the flesh was weak. Perhaps the Orphir team felt that with a four goal lead they did not require to take the second leg of the tie too seriously. At all events, when the game began it was a collection of wan-faced, bleary-eyed Orphir footballers who reeled to their positions, and Stenwick romped to a 6-1 victory, Orphir's one goal being scored by a Stenwick defender.

This brought Stenwick into the semi-final, but it was freely prophesied that this was as far as they would go, for they were now to encounter Holm, a cup-fighting team of formidable reputation. Even the Stenwick players were pessimistic, but not so Godfrey Ritch. Roundly denouncing the defeatists, he put his faith in the glorious uncertainty of football. Later it struck him that faith was perhaps not enough, and so he arranged for the delivery, to each of the six Holm players he most feared, of a parcel of sooan scones made to a special recipe.

When the Stenwick team arrived at Holm for the first match of the tie the following evening they were pleasantly surprised to discover that Holm's six best men were unavailable owing to mysterious attacks of food poisoning. Stenwick won 3-1, thanks to a brilliant hat-trick by their outside-left, Alan Morton Learmonth, who, in the rare intervals when he is sober, is a performer second to none in Orkney. Holm arrived at Stenwick for the return at full strength, and confident of wiping out the arrears, but they were met by a home team which was determined to hold on to its lead. Throughout the game the entire Stenwick team remained wedged in its own goal area, presenting a solid wall of flesh to every effort by the opposition. When the final whistle blew, Holm had succeeded in scoring only one goal, and that from a penalty conceded by Armstrong Tait, who had put his hands to a cannonball drive to save himself from annihilation. Battered black and blue but triumphant, the Stenwick team left the field to an ovation from their supporters that was heard by a bird watcher on the Brough of Birsay. Two nights later Stenwick learned that Harray had defeated Firth in the other semi-final. The stage was thus set for a cup-final between neighbouring parishes, between whom, whether on the football field or anywhere else, relations have been rather less cordial than those existing between Messrs Churchill and Attlee.

○ ○ ○ ○ ○ ○

"Weel," said Tristram Mainland, "whit dis thoo think? Hiv wae a chance tae win?"

His query was addressed to old Godfrey Ritch, who had been watching the team at practice with a critical eye. The time was two nights before the final.

"A chance," ejaculated the veteran. "Of coorse thoo his a

chance. Thoo'll bitt Harray intae a cocked hat. Dinno tell me thoo're no confeedent, boy."

"Whit wey shid I be confeedent?" asked Tristram. "Thoo ken as weel as me that wur been deshed lucky tae reach the final."

"Luck idsel niver took ony team in the final o' ony cup," replied Godfrey sagely. "Thir wis noathing lucky aboot id when thoo bitt Holm in the first game o' the semi-final."

"Wis thir no?" asked Tristram. "If six o' thir players hidno hin food poisonin' wae wid niver hiv smelt id. Wis yin no luck?"

"Niver a bit o' id," replied the veteran, with a crafty grin. "I wur responseeble for them gittan food poisonin'." And he explained how it had been done.

Tristram looked at him with eyebrows contracted. Though he has few scruples about how he disables an opponent on the field of play, Tristram is sportsman enough to disapprove of some of the methods taken by the president of the club to ensure victory.

"If wae kinno win be fair play," he said austerely, "id's better tae no win at all."

"Dirt," retorted Godfrey. "Thoo're ould-fashioned, boy. Win be fair play, indeed. I niver hard the like. Onywey, yin team o' wur's will niver win be fair play. Wur defence is fer fae soond, an' wur haff-line is no gret, except for Alan Morton Learmonth. As sheur as a'm livin' the team seems tae git warse, an' no' better."

"An' yet," sneered Tristram, "thoo're expectin' iss tae bitt Harray."

"Thoo're gaun tae bitt Harray," declared Godfrey with emphasis. "Be crook or be hook."

"Hid'll be be crook if thoo his onything tae dae wi'd," grunted Tristram. "But thoo'll no find id aisy tae work ony dirty wark wi' Harray. They ken thee ower weel."

"Maybe ay, an' maybe no," snickered Godfrey. He stroked his luxuriant whiskers, and mused: "I hiv an aafil feeleen that Harray is gaun tae be short o' some o' thir ster players on Setterday night."

"More food poisonin', no doot?"

Godfrey looked pained.

"No no, boy, I niver work the sam' kepper twice. I think a'll cheust tak' me ker an' go for a peedie run aroond Harray, an' see whit's tae be seen. An' as for thee, boy, go back on the field an' keep thee team herd at practeece, for even if Harray shid be short o' some o' their best men, thoo'll still hiv a herd chob tae win them."

The frowning Tristram watched him get into his ancient car and drive off, and then trotted back on to the football pitch to whip up his players to more vigorous efforts.

O O O O O O O

Crossing the parish boundary between Stenwick and Harray, Godfrey cruised quietly along, darting searching glances to left and right. At length he emitted a grunt of satisfaction as, passing the farm steading of Gloup, he observed a massive figure on a ladder, apparently engaged in making some repairs to the roof of the byre. It was Goliath Flett, ace defender in the Harray team, a veritable Colossus of a player, standing six feet six in his socks, and weighing perhaps a few ounces less than the bull Bluebell of Quoydunt. Goliath's salutary methods of dealing with opposing forwards have kept the Orkney Hospital Board busy ever since its institution, and he represented the chief stumbling block to a Stenwick victory in the final.

Godfrey stopped the car, got out, and ambled across to the byre.

"Ay boy," he greeted, "thoo're busy."

The gigantic Goliath glanced down, but with no welcoming smile.

"Whit dis thoo want?" he growled.

"Noathing, boy. I wur cheust passin' in me ker, an' I thowt I wid come an' spick tae thee."

"Weel a'm no wantin' tae spick tae thee," replied Goliath, "so thoo kin clear fae here."

"Er thoo feelin' fit for the match?" asked Godfrey.

"I am hid," said Goliath, with a wicked grin, "an' thoo kin tell thee centre-forward tae mak' his will afore Setterday night."

"A'll deu hid," replied Godfrey, and turned to walk away. By accident or design the handle of his walking stick caught in one of the rungs of the ladder, and it tottered perilously.

Goliath emitted a howl of alarm.

"Boy, watch whit thoo're daein'. Thoo'll hiv me doon."

"Geud," said Godfrey, "me staff's catched in thee ladder." He gave it a vigorous wrench. The ladder heeled over, and to the accompaniment of a despairing wail from Goliath, it crashed to the ground with an impact that made windows rattle in their frames over a wide area.

Godfrey rushed to the assistance of the fallen giant.

"My mercy," he cried, "a'm aafil sorry, boy. Er thoo hurt?"

He waited in some anxiety for the answer as Goliath struggled painfully to his feet, and felt his various limbs, emitting a whoop of pain as he put his weight on his right leg.

"Me knee's twisted," he groaned. "I doot a'm oot o' the final."

"Boy, that's aafil," said Godfrey, but the sparkle in his aged eyes belied his sympathy. Goliath gave him a murderous glare.

"Thoo clumsy ould clurt, id's all thee falt. Could thoo no watch whit thoo wur daein' wi' thee staff? I hiv a geud mind tae knock thee block off. Clear fae here afore I dae id." He hobbled menacingly towards the veteran, who withdrew briskly to his car and drove off in high glee. That, he told himself, had effectively disposed of one of the Harray stars.

Entering Dounby he had another stroke of luck. At the cross-roads, just beside the hotel, stood a group of four youths, in earnest conversation. Three of the four he recognised as being members of the Harray football team, and leading members at that, Crispin Flett, Figaro Flett and Arbuthnot Flett. Jamming his foot on the accelerator he swerved sharply to the right, and at the last moment blew a furious blast on his horn, which was enough to throw the four youths into a panic but not enough to give them time to get out of the way.

Figaro Flett, Arbuthnot Flett and the fourth member of

"Me knee's twisted," moaned Flett. "I doot a'm oot o' the final."

the group, Aneurin Bichan, went down before the car like shot rabbits. Crispin Flett, with a kangaroo bound, managed to get clear, but not clear enough, for Godfrey, instantly slamming his car into reverse, bowled him over neck and crop.

The veteran of Mucklegutter, simulating the deepest regret, got out to survey the stricken field and tot up the casualties. Figaro Flett had a broken ankle, Arbuthnot a broken rib, and Crispin Flett a broken jaw. Mentally Godfrey rubbed his hands with satisfaction. The results could scarcely have been better. All three were clearly hors de combat for the final. It was a pity that Aneurin Bichan was not a player as well, as he looked in distinctly poor shape.

A crowd had collected and Godfrey found himself the object of some hostile comment, particularly from a number of Harray football supporters, who were of the opinion that he should be taken and pitched into the Loch of Harray, preferably with his car tied round his neck. Just as steps were on the point of being taken to carry this intention out the local police officer arrived at a run, and lynch law was averted.

It was a smiling Godfrey Ritch who drove out of Dounby some fifteen minutes later. He had been charged with careless driving, but he regarded the possibility of a £3 fine and endorsement of his licence a small price to pay for having got rid, at one blow, of three of the Harray team.

Nor was he finished yet. On the homeward run to Stenwick he pulled up at the garage kept by Clerihew Flett, the Harray team's go-ahead right-half, and under pretext of getting Clerihew to look at his carburettor, managed to drop a large and heavy crowbar on the unsuspecting mechanic's foot. He apologised profusely and drove briskly away, leaving Clerihew hopping agonisedly round a petrol pump.

Three-quarters of an hour after he had left it he arrived back at the Stenwick football pitch with the heartening information for the team that when Harray took the field on Saturday night they were almost certain to do so without five of their key players.

"Some dirty wark on thee pairt, likely," commented Tristram Mainland grimly.

"Not id," replied the veteran, with a show of injured innocence. "Cheust wen or two regrettable acceedents. Acceedents will happen, thoo ken."

"They happen when thoo're aboothands all right," grunted Tristram.

○ ○ ○ ○ ○ ○

In Dounby the following evening a special meeting of the Harray Football Club was called. It was presided over by the president of the Club, Pluto Flett, and it was evident to all present, from Pluto's black brow and glittering eyes, that he was in no pleasant temper.

"Weel," he rapped out. "Thoo'll be winderin' whit this meetin' is aboot. A'll tell thee. Thoo'll be aware, no doot, that five o' wur team is been crocked?"

"Yaas," said Mordecai Clouston, the vice-president. "I hard thir hid been some acceedents."

"Acceedents," raved Flett. "Thir wis noathing acceedental aboot whit happened tae ony o' them. Godfrey Ritch wur responseeble for the lot. He knocked Goliath Flett aff o' a ledder, he ran doon Figaro Flett, an' Arbuthnot Flett, an' Crispin Flett wi' his ker, an' he drapped a gret crowber on Clerihew Flett's feet."

"Might id wur acceedents, all the sam'," observed Mordecai Clouston.

Pluto looked at the vice-president from bloodshot eyes.

"Boy," he grated, "if thoo say id wur acceedents again, a'll tak' me stick an' gie thee the best cloor on the side o' the heid that thoo're iver gotten. If id wur acceedents a'm the Prime Meeneester. Godfrey Ritch," and his voice rose to a scream as he uttered the hated name. "Godfrey Ritch is deun iss a mony a time in the past, an' he's deun iss again noo. He cam' tae Harray last night tae crock wur players an' mak' iss go in the final wi' wur team haff-strength, an' he's din id. An' the question wur here tae decide is, whit er wae gaun tae deu?"

There was a long silence, broken by one Abednego Stockan, who gloomily observed:

"Weel, whit kin wae deu?"

"Wae kin all go fae here tae ould Ritch's hoose," shouted a hot-blooded youth named Midas Moodie, "an' draig him oot an' fling him in the Loch o' Stenwick."

"Yin's weel spocken Midas," said Pluto Flett approvingly, "an' wae'll maybe dae hid teu, bit whit I wur meanin' wur whit er wae gaun tae deu tae the Stenwick team, tae mak' sheur they'll no win iss?"

"They'll no win iss," scoffed Mordecai Clouston. "Even if wae shid be short o' ten o' wur regulars Stenwick will no bitt iss. Thir hoppless. I saa them playin' Shapinsay, an' Shapinsay wisno gret, but Stenwick wis warse."

"They won, though," pointed out Abednego Stockan.

"Yaas, for Shapinsay hid haff thir players awey wi' mumps, an' even then Stenwick hid the luck o' Ould Nick."

"Yin wur in the second roond," Abednego Stockan reninded him. "Thir better noo. They bitt Holm 3-1 at Holm, in the semi-final."

"Bit id wurno Holm's full team," retorted Clouston. "Haff a dizzen o' the Holm sters wisno playin', the wey they hid food poisonin'."

"I hard aboot hid," said Pluto Flett, "an' id's me belief that Godfrey Ritch wur responsible for yin."

"I widno be surprised," agreed Stockan. "Id's cheust like wen o' his tricks."

"Wae hiv noathing tae worry aboot," declared Mordecai Clouston. "Yin Stenwick team couldno bitt an egg. They cheust hiv wan geud player, thir ootside-left, Alan Morton Learmonth. Tristram Mainland is no bed at centre-half, bit Learmonth's thir ster."

"Exactly," said Pluto Flett, "an' I suggest that Learmonth be removed fae the Stenwick team, an' then wae'll be sheur tae win."

"An' whit wey er thoo gaun tae remove him fae the team?" inquired Polonius Garson.

"The sam' wey as ould Ritch is removed five o' wur players," retorted Pluto, with a wolfish grin.

"I dinno agree," bluntly declared Mordecai Clouston. "Wae kin bitt Stenwick withoot this dirty wark."

"Weel, I wid say the sam'," replied Flett, "if id wur ony

ither team bit Stenwick, bit luk hoo affen wur suffered fae
Stenwick's chukery-packery. Wur let them awey wi' id fer
ower long. An' mind on, wae kinno be sheur o' winnin'
except Learmonth's oot o' thir team. Hends up all that think
wae shid remove Learmonth."

The hand of everyone in the meeting, with the exception
of Mordecai Clouston, shot up.

"Cairried," declared Pluto. "Noo Midas Moodie, thoo
his a motter bike. Tak' Septimus Stanger up ahint thee an'
go tae Stenwick. Thoo kens whar Learmonth steys, dis thoo
no?"

Midas nodded.

"Weel, Septimus kin cry him oot tae the road, an' as
seun as he sets feet on the road, Midas, run him doon wi'
thee bike. No ower herd, for wae dinno want tae kill the
fella, cheust enough tae brak his leg, or twist his ankle. Is
that clear?"

Midas Moodie and Septimus Stanger nodded briskly.

Within three minutes the roar of Midas Moodie's motor
cycle could be heard receding in the distance.

Abednego Stockan gave Pluto a look such as one of
Napoleon's marshals might have bestowed on his chief.

"Boy, Pluto," he said admiringly, "thoo're the wen for
ould Ritch."

Pluto preened himself. "Yaas," he agreed, "I hiv all me
wits aboot me."

But alas for Pluto Flett, when it comes to matching wits
against Godfrey Ritch he is as a child trying to outdo a
Machiavelli. Godfrey had foreseen the possibility that
Harray would attempt retaliation and had arranged that the
residence of every Stenwick player was guarded by a patrol
of supporters.

Less than twenty minutes after they had set out, an
extremely chagrined Midas Moodie and Septimus Stanger
were back in Harray, recounting to Pluto Flett how, as soon
as they had reached the neighbourhood of the Learmonth
homestead they had been surrounded by hostile Sten-
wickians, had had their posteriors soundly kicked, and had
been instructed to get out and not show their faces in the
parish again for at least twenty-four hours.

It was a bitter pill for Pluto Flett, and he chewed his moustache with frustrated fury.

"Bit a'm no deun yet," he vowed. "Cheust wett. Learmonth will no turn oot for Stenwick next night."

o o o o o o

The Parish Cup final, as most readers are no doubt aware, is played at the Bignold Park, Kirkwall, on the evening of County Show day. Thus players and supporters of both teams left for the town early in the morning, for many of them were required to be of service at the Show, either in handling stock exhibits for their employers, or officiating as stewards on behalf of the Orkney Agricultural Society at the various rings.

Alan Morton Learmonth, whose job it was to drag black-polled cattle from pen to ring and vice versa for his employer, Willie Budge of Snortquoy, had two narrow escapes during the forenoon. But for the quick-wittedness of Peedie Tam of Quoydunt, who hauled him out of the way just in time, he would have been run down by a float, recklessly driven by Abednego Stockan. Later a bottle carelessly thrown from the balcony of the pavilion grazed his ear while he was entering the tea tent.

Little did Learmonth suspect that these were deliberate attempts to incapacitate him for the football match, engineered by Pluto Flett. During the afternoon, while he was watching the sports programme, Pluto Flett in person accosted him and invited him into the licensed tent for a dram. Flett well knew Learmonth's weakness for strong drink, and once he got him into the tent he counted on plying him with whisky until the little winger was in no condition to be a menace on the football field, except to his own team. Unluckily for Flett, the possibility that Learmonth would not be able to resist the lure of the licensed tent had been anticipated by Godfrey Ritch. When Flett and his companion gained the doorway of the marquee they encountered the grim faces of Boris Corsie and Gabriel Stout. These two, detailed for the purpose of denying their left-winger access to liquor until after the match, firmly and none too gently separated him from the Harray president and escorted him to a lemonade stall.

A touch of desperation appeared in Pluto Flett's expression, but he had not yet shot his last bolt.

Stenwick are one of the clubs which pander to the modern notion that footballers must be carefully nursed from all exertion before appearing on the field of play. Thus a bus had been engaged to convey them from the hotel where they had tea to the Bignold Park. As the members of the team, stripped for action, walked from the hotel to the bus, Alan Morton Learmonth was stopped by a remarkably pretty girl with a jaunty beret on her head, and lips painted to a vivid scarlet.

"Boy," she said, putting her hand on his arm, "thoo're me favourite player. I hopp thoo win."

She was a complete stranger to Learmonth, but his is the view that the advances of a handsome wench should never be discouraged.

"Wae'll win all right," he said with an ingratiating grin. "A'll see thoo're no disappointed."

"Will thoo let me gie thee a peedie kess for luck," she inquired.

"Boyo," cried Learmonth, and opened his arms.

"No here, though," she objected. "Come up this closs, whar thir'll nobody see iss."

She backed up the close, and the Stenwick outside-left followed with alacrity.

"Noo," she said, stopping opposite a dark doorway, "nobody kin see iss here. Oppen thee mooth an' shut thee eyes."

Learmonth did so, but what followed was somewhat contrary to his expectations. No pair of luscious lips was pressed against his mouth, but a large and not too sweet-smelling hand was clamped over it, an arm was hooked tightly round his neck, two more arms were fastened round his waist, and he was hustled, struggling furiously, into the dark doorway. He opened his eyes to gaze into the grinning triumphant faces of Midas Moodie and Septimus Stanger, and that was the last he saw before a dirty sack was pulled down over his head.

Mimosa Flett, her role of femme fatale completed, tripped gracefully back down the close and into the street. No-one appeared to have noticed the little incident, and apparently Learmonth had not even been missed as yet for the footballers' bus was moving away. Mimosa was the daughter of Caliban Flett, a brother of Pluto, though long resident in Kirkwall. It was, reflected Mimosa, as she headed for the nearest chip shop, a peculiar affair, but she was always glad to assist her Uncle Pluto, however odd his requests, especially when he backed them up with a ten bob bonus.

o o o o o o

The bus drew up in front of the pavilion, and players and officials tumbled out. It was still five minutes to kick-off time. The team trotted towards the pitch to pass the remaining few minutes with some practice at kicking for goal, which, as some supporters agreed, they could certainly do with.

Godfrey Ritch, who was watching them, suddenly let out a howl.

"Thir's cheust ten players there. Whar's missin'?"

"Geud goad," cried Eustace Rosie, the vice-president of the club, "thoo're right, Godfrey. Thir's cheust ten indeed. Learmonth's no there."

"Dorrin on him," grated Godfrey, "whar kin he be?" He shouted Tristram Mainland over, and demanded to know what had become of the outside-left.

"I wur sheur he cam' in the bus," said Tristram, puzzled. "Onywey, he cam' oot o' the hotel wi' iss, for wae made sheur wark he wurno gettan in the ber. Might he's up in the pavilion."

Eustace Rosie scampered into the pavilion. In the Harray dressing-room he could hear Pluto Flett giving some last-minute advice, mainly based on the dictum that if the players were unable to get the man they should at least get the ball. In the other dressing-room there was no sign of Alan Morton Learmonth, and he returned to Godfrey with the unpleasant news. Godfrey threw his hands towards Heaven.

"The peedie whalp," he raved, "he's likely got in the ber somewey an' will be drinkin' himsel gueshless. Eustace, boy, tak' the bus an' go doon the toon, an' git him here if thoo hiv tae draig him be the hair o' the heid."

Eustace did so, but in five minutes he was back with the news that Learmonth was not in the ber, and had not been in the ber at all.

He, Eustace, had spoken to a bystander who remembered seeing a small footballer speaking to a girl at the close end, but what had happened to him after that the bystander did not know.

The referee's whistle blew a peremptory blast from the pitch, and the Harray team came clattering out of the pavilion, followed, at a more sedate pace, by Pluto Flett and sundry of the club officials.

"Boy, Pluto," said Godfrey, "kin wae no deley the start a peedie bit? Wur ootside-left is gone a-missin'."

A triumphant grin flickered for an instant at the corner of Flett's mouth before he answered: "Id kinno be deun. If thoo're short o' a man thoo kin play wi' ten men or pit on a reserve. Wur no deleyin' the game for thee."

With a sudden flash of insight Godfrey knew that this man was responsible for the non-appearance of Alan Morton Learmonth. He drew back, pointing a shaking, accusatory finger at Pluto Flett. "This is thee wark, Flett," he shouted. "Whit er thoo din wi' Learmonth?"

"I dinno ken whit thoo're spickan aboot," snapped Flett, "bit all I kin say is that if thoo're lost Learmonth id's cheust the price o' thee for the wark thoo're worked on wur team." Smugly he added, "I wid say id's a chudgement on Stenwick," and, pushing past the veteran, he headed for the pitch.

Godfrey stared after him, half-minded to deal him a cloor on the lug with his staff, but he refrained, postponing that pleasure until later. Simmering with fury he swung round, and his eye fell on Nathaniel Swanney.

"Swenney," he barked, "wur a man short. Thoo'll hiv tae play."

"Bit—bit a'm no muckle yeuse," protested Swanney.

Godfrey disillusioned him. "No muckle yeuse? Thoo're

no yeuse at all, bit maybe thoo'll be better than noathing. Thir's a chersey, an' shorts an' beuts in the bus. Git crackin'."

"Boy, boy," muttered Eustace Rosie, "hid's a peur day when Nathaniel Swenney his tae play for Stenwick. I doot wur had id."

"If Harray wins iss," ground out Godfrey, "a'll tear Pluto Flett fae ither wi' me bare hends."

o o o o o o

To the accompaniment of a roar from three thousand throats the game began, and for the first five or ten minutes the Stenwick defence was hard pressed, but fortunately for the blood pressure of the Stenwick supporters the ineptness of their team's rearguard was more than matched by the cluelessness of the Harray forward line, in which the three substitutes for Figaro Flett, Arbuthnot Flett and Crispin Flett were giving no indication that they had ever played football before. Nevertheless the Stenwick keeper, Gabriel Stout, was in luck's way when he got his face in front of a humdinger from the Harray outside-right, Vulcan Budge, though Gabriel, as he dazedly endeavoured to ascertain whether his head was still attached to his shoulders, probably wondered where the luck came in.

"Here comes Nathaniel Swenney," said Eustace Rosie. "Wae hiv eliven men noo, at ony ritt."

Godfrey glanced sourly at the gangling figure of Swanney as he took up his position on the wing. There, the veteran reflected, but for the dastardly intervention of Pluto Flett, went Alan Morton Learmonth. He noted with an inward sneer that Swanney had his boots on the wrong feet, but did nor trouble to inform him of the fact, considering that it would make little difference to his shooting in any case.

Having resisted twenty minutes of pressure Stenwick broke away on the attack. Diogenes Corrigall, Goliath Flett's replacement, proved grossly unequal to the task of intercepting a pass by Stanley Marwick, and Nathaniel Swanney, galloping in from the wing like a lame giraffe, had presented to him a glorious opportunity.

"Noo's thee chance, Swenney. Shoot," screamed Godfrey Ritch.

Nathaniel shot, with his left foot—but his right boot—and scooped the ball grotesquely in the direction of the corner flag.

Godfrey, after hurling an epithet at Swanney which cannot be reproduced here, covered his face with his hands, and groaned, "If Peedie Learmonth hid been there it wid hiv been a goal."

Eustace Rosie glanced at the sky and remarked, "Id luks like comin' doon a mist." And indeed a thick white blanket was rolling down over Wideford Hill.

Heartened by this escape, Harray bore down on the Stenwick goal like wolves on the fold, and only a desperate tackle by Peedie Tam of Quoydunt prevented Vulcan Budge scoring at point blank range. But the referee decided that a tackle which had involved clutching Budge around the waist and throwing him headlong could not be permitted, and, blowing his whistle, he pointed to the penalty spot. Stenwick protests were of no avail. In a deadly hush Diogenes Corrigall stepped up to take the spot-kick and battered the ball ten feet over the crossbar.

The Stenwick fans howled their relief, while Pluto Flett gibbered with rage and nearly burst a blood vessel trying to put his feelings towards the crestfallen Corrigall into words.

Five minutes from half-time Stenwick had another escape, thanks to the quick wits of their linesman, Geordie Manson. The dangerous Vulcan Budge dashed in from the wing and cracked a terrific volley into the back of the net, but Geordie Manson had anticipated the move and was frantically waving his flag for offside ere the leather had come to rest.

Once again Pluto Flett's blood vessels creaked under the strain imposed on them, as the referee upheld Geordie's claim.

When the second half commenced mist was rolling across the pitch, and soon it had become so thick that the players were visible only as dim outlines, and it was impossible to tell one player from another. This was responsible for the goal which Harray scored after fifteen minutes. Tristram Mainland, who had been playing a great game, successfully tackled an opponent and slipped the ball to what he thought was the figure of Armstrong Tait to clear. To his speechless consternation it was not Armstrong Tait at all, but the Harray inside-right, Giles Hourston, who promptly crashed the ball past a helpless Gabriel Stout.

Pluto Flett relaxed with a sigh of satisfaction. "That'll dae iss," he remarked. "Stenwick will niver score in the days o' man."

○ ○ ○ ○ ○ ○

And indeed it looked as if Pluto was right. What little team-work Stenwick had been showing had vanished completely with the added complication of the mist, and passes went astray with grievous regularity. As the minutes ticked away the gloom on the faces of Godfrey Ritch and Eustace Rosie deepened.

"Luk at yin," muttered Godfrey thickly as a figure which he thought he could identify as Nathaniel Swanney kicked the ball from two yards' range into the hands of the keeper.

"Hoo long tae go noo?" asked Eustace.

"Quarter o' an 'oor," replied Godfrey, glancing at his watch.

"Wur had id," said Eustace, shaking his head.

Someone tapped Godfrey on the back. He turned irritably, and nearly jumped out of his boots. Alan Morton Learmonth stood there, hair tousled, face grimy, wearing a raincoat over his football kit.

"Whar the dickens er thoo been?" snarled the veteran. "Thoo peedie whalp, thoo're lost iss the game."

"Id wurno me falt," said the little winger, "A'm been kidnapped."

Godfrey's eyes blazed. "I thowt thir wis dirty wark," he gritted. "Pluto Flett, no doot."

"Id wur Midas Moodie an' Septimus Stanger, as a metter o' fact," said Learmonth, "bit likely id wur Flett's orders. A'm been sittin wi' a gag in me mooth, an' me feet an' hends tied, an' a seck ower me heid for the last oor an' a haff, an' likely I wid hiv been sittin' yet, bit a fella wur passin' an' hard me keekin' on the fleur an' let me oot. Whit's happenin' here?"

"Wur lossin'," moaned Eustace. "Harray's winnin' iss wen-noathing. Nathaniel Swenney is playin' in thee pliss, an' makkin' the most aafil heggis o' id that thoo iver saa. Whit a peety that thoo hidno been here at the start, boy. Id's ower litt noo."

But Godfrey burst out, with a gleam in his eye: "Whit dis thoo mean, ower litt? Learmonth, tak' aff thee cott an' get oot on the field. Thoo kin win this game for iss yet."

"Bit my mighty," Eustace spluttered, "thoo kinno dae yin. Id'll no be allooed."

"Whar's gaun tae ken?" demanded Godfrey. "Whar's thee wits, boy? In this mist thoo kinno tell wen player fae anither, an' Harray will niver notteece that there's twelve Stenwick men on the pitch."

"Bit the spectetters—" objected Eustace.

"Will thoo stoop?" snapped Godfrey. He gestured around him. "All the spectetters aroond iss is Stenwick fock. They'll no let on. Queek, Learmonth, on thoo go, an' dinno deley langer, for it cheust wants ten meenits o' time up."

Learmonth, slippping off his coat, dashed on to the field and became just another shape in the mist. Presently the ball came to him. Deftly outwitting three men in a bewildering burst of speed, he slammed it from twenty yards past the Harray keeper.

All square, and five minutes to go. The pace was hectic.

"Whar scored yin goal?" asked Pluto Flett, of his neighbours.

"Weel," replied one of them, "id cam' fae the left, so id wur sheurly Nathaniel Swenney, though I didno think id wur in Swenney tae score a goal like yin."

"Id lukked peedier than Swenney tae me," grunted Flett. "If I didno ken—" He broke off, and followed the play with a growing apprehension.

Four minutes to go. Three minutes. Two minutes. Once again Alan Morton Learmonth collected the ball. He was unmarked, for the Harray defence was under the impression that it had every opposing forward covered. Closing in on

goal at terrific speed, he let go a volley that the Harray
goalkeeper never saw until he rummaged for it in the meshes
of the net.

Swiftly Learmonth dashed off the field, donned his coat
and took his position beside the now jubilant Godfrey and
Eustace, while the Stenwick defence safely played out the
remaining seconds. As the final whistle went, the Stenwick
team gathered round an astonished Nathaniel Swanney,
carried him shoulder-high off the field, and congratulated
him all the way to the pavilion on his two match-winning
goals.

Godfrey whacked a mortified Pluto Flett on the
shoulder.

"Id cheust shaws thee, boy," he said, "dirty wark niver
peys. Thoo kidnapped wur ster, but wae won thee wantin'
him."

Pluto Flett stared hard at the grinning Alan Morton
Learmonth. He said nothing, but he walked away thinking
long, long thoughts, which became even longer when he got
to the Harray dressing-room, and overheard a defender
comment ruefully, "Thoo wid hiv thowt yin Stenwick team
hid haff a dizzan forwards in the last ten meenits, wi' yin
pressure they pat on."

Pluto sat down and a bitter smile wreathed his lips. Not
for the first time he realised that to put anything over on
Godfrey Ritch one has to get up very early in the morning.

Bluebell of Quoydunt

If you come to Orkney and ask the inhabitants what it is that makes the name of Orkney famous throughout the civilised world the chances are that the answer will vary according to the district in which the question is put.

In Kirkwall you will almost certainly be told, "St Magnus Cathedral," and in Stromness, " the motor vessel St Ola." In Holm the answer will probably be "The Churchill Barriers," in Deerness "The Gloup," in Hoy "The Dwarfie Stone," in Stenness "The Standing Stones," in Papa Westray "St Tredwell's Loch," in Finstown "The Pomona," and in South Ronaldsay "The Murray Arms."

Nowhere, however, will there be a more emphatic reply than you will get in Stenwick, and the reply there will be "Bluebell o' Quoydunt."

Bluebell, that noble pure-bred Aberdeen-Angus bull, is regarded by the inhabitants of Stenwick rather as Queen Victoria was regarded by the people of 19th-century England, with pride, affection, and veneration. He is an institution, an apotheosis of bullhood, a symbol of Stenwick's pre-eminent agricultural fertility. Though long past the age at which a bull is generally regarded as being in his prime, Bluebell has declined neither in the majesty of his appearance nor in those characteristics with which a bull is associated. Despite the fierce competition of younger animals the finest calves born in the West Mainland are still those for which Bluebell has been responsible, by a long chalk, and it is said by cattlemen that a cow's eyes will light up, and she will moo with pleasurable anticipation, at the prospect of being mated with the great bull of Quoydunt. Bluebell, in fact, is a sort of Errol Flynn of the bovine world.

Visiting farmers from the south—and there have been more and more of these since the pilgrimage to Quoydunt has become an essential part of an agriculturalist's education —seeing Bluebell for the first time generally recoil in disbelief, and then, convinced that this magnificent specimen is real, and no mere figment of their imagination, remove their hats and fall to their knees in tribute. Their next reaction is to fumble for their cheque-books and offer Bluebell's owner, Chohn Clouston, fabulous sums if he will sell. But Chohn smilingly refuses all offers, telling them, and with perfect truth, that he would sooner think of selling his wife than of selling Bluebell, and the visitors return home, bemused, wondering, and envious, sad at heart to think that this pearl among bulls can never be theirs, yet uplifted in spirit, like men whose eyes have beheld great miracles.

o o o o o o

It was the day before the Dounby Show, and Chohn had Bluebell out in the little yard behind the byre, brushing him down and generally putting the finishing touches to his appearance. The task was somewhat in the nature of gilding the lily, for it was impossible that the great bull could be in a condition of greater perfection than he already was. However, it gave Chohn something to do, and there was nothing about the farm which he found more congenial. Indeed, the attention he devoted to Bluebell caused something of a poor view to be taken of him by his wife Chessie, and his employees, Mansie and Peedie Tam, who felt that they were required to shoulder an unfairly large burden of the ordinary farm routine.

As he wielded the brush, slowly and rhythmically, Chohn talked to Bluebell.

"Weel boy," he said, "hid's the Show again the morn, an' thoo'll sheur tae git the championship, an' weel thoo'll desserve id, for thir's no anither aneemil in Orkney fit tae luk at thee. Whit dis thoo think, boy? Er thoo confeedent?"

Bluebell, naturally, did not reply, for wonderful animal as he is, his talents do not include the power of speech. His left ear twitched, as an indication that he knew he was being spoken to, but his large, grave eyes remained fixed on the infinite.

"Whit er thoo thinkin' aboot, boy?" Chohn inquired,

"Er thoo thinkin' aboot all the fock whar's gaun tae admire thee the morn?"

Bluebell twitched his ear again, but what his thoughts were remained obscure. He might have been meditating on the transience of earthly glory, the insignificance of trophies and championships against the more profound problems of life, and the shape of things to come in the bovine hereafter. Or perhaps his thoughts were on a more mundane plane. Perhaps he was wondering when his supper was going to be served up, or whether there would be any attractive cows at the showyard the following day. At any rate his expression was inscrutable, as inscrutable as that of an Orkneyman listening to the wheedlings of a candidate at a General Election.

Willie Budge of Snortquoy, Chohn's close friend and neighbour, entered the steading, leaned over the gate of the yard, and surveyed Bluebell with an approving eye.

"He's lukkin' weel, Chohn," he commented.

"Ay is he," agreed Chohn.

"He's a gret bull," pursued Willie, coming into the yard and walking slowly round Bluebell, as a visitor to London walks round St Paul's Cathedral, in mingled wonder and reverence. Willie saw Bluebell practically every day of his life, but he never tired of the spectacle.

"A gret bull indeed," said Chohn.

"The grettest bull in the West Mainland," said Willie.

"In Orkney," corrected Chohn, with a glance of reproof.

"Yaas yaas," said Willie, "that's whit I meant."

Chohn continued brushing and Willie continued his circumnambulation.

"Id's a sed thowt," observed Willie at length, "that the day o' the bull is gettan aboot deun."

Chohn stopped brushing and looked at him sharply.

"Whit's that? The day o' the bull gettan deun. Whit dirt's this thoo're sayin'?"

"Hid's no dirt," said Willie, a trifle nettled. "Thoo'll be hard o' arteeficial insemeenation?"

"Oh yin!" Chohn made a contemptuous gesture. He had indeed heard of artificial insemination, as he had heard of a great deal of new-fangled claptrap, like atom bombs, television, and psycho-analysis, but he had dismissed it as unlikely ever to come within his orbit of experience.

"Hid's all very weel sayin' 'Oh yin'," said Willie, "bit the day's comin' when id'll be deun all ower, an' then bulls will be for no more yeuse."

"Niver in Orkney," said Chohn.

"Thoo're wrong there," said Willie grimly, "for id's been deun in Orkney already, an' thoo'll see the ootcome at the show the morn."

Chohn looked at Willie as if he could not believe his ears.

"Dis thoo mean tae tell me that thir's an Orkney fermer tried arteeficial insemeenation? Whar is this whalp?"

"Hid's wen o' thee closest neebors. Cuthbert Harcus o' Rumtodly. He his a grand peedie calf entered for the show the morn. Id's fae his coo Angeline whit wur runner-up tae Bluebell two 'ear ago. He ferly thinks id's gaun tae bitt Bluebell the morn, an' feth, boy, Bluebell will hiv a herd chob if he's gaun tae win id."

"Id's the first a'm hard aboot this," said Chohn, "bit of coorse Harcus widno tell me, the wey wur no on spickan terms."

"Thir's no mony dis ken aboot id," said Willie. "Harcus is a gey hidden thing at ony time, an' he's been keepin' id dark, for he's ferly lippenin' tae spring id on thee the morn an' tak' the cup tae Rumtodly. I cheust hard aboot id the day mesel, an' id wur young Harcus whar let id slip oot."

"Did thoo see the calf?"

"I did hid, though Hector wurno keen on me daein' id. Id's a topper. A heifer calf, no ferly a year ould."

Chohn looked puzzled. Rumtodly had no stock bull, and he had heard of no activities of this sort in connection with Harcus's cattle.

"Whar's ids sire?" he asked.

"That's cheust id," cried Willie. "Id's whit a'm been tellin' thee. Id hid no sire. Except thoo kin say id wur sired be a hippeedermic needle."

"A whit?"

"A hippeedermic needle. Id wur sired be arteeficial insemeenation. A fella sheurly cam' up fae the sooth an' did id, an' Hector said id cost his fether a bonny penny, bit thir's noathing ould Harcus will no trey tae bitt thee at the show."

Chohn's ruddy face purpled with indignation, not directed against Rumtodly, but against the principle of artificial insemination generally.

"Id's disgusteen," he shouted. "Id's an ootrage against nature. Whit on earth will they trey next?"

Willie shrugged his shoulders. "I wid say the sam' as thee boy, bit thir aye up tae some new keppers, an' thir's no muckle we kin deu aboot id. Id's progress, they say."

"Progress." Chohn spat out the word. "Yin's no whit I wid call id."

Willie prudently did not ask what Chohn would call it, for he had no wish to listen to expressions unbecoming to the ears of an elder of the kirk. After a short silence he went on: "When it gets aroond the morn thir'll be a lot watchin' the ootcome, an' if this calf o' Rumtodly wins the cup id'll be a big boost for arteeficial insemeenation here. I widno say bit thoo might loss some o' Bluebell's customers."

Chohn snorted contemptuously. "If they wid rether hiv thir coos sired be a needle than be Bluebell they kin hed gaun. If I wis a coo I ken whit wid be me choice."

"An' mine," said Willie emphatically. "Still, thir's a lot goes be whar wins a show championship. I hopp Bluebell wins."

Willie took his leave, and for some time Chohn remained in the yard, revolving in his mind what Willie had told him. He addressed Bluebell musingly: "Boy, whit wid thoo say if I pat thee on the scraphaep, an' bowt a hippeedermic needle in thee pliss?"

Could Bluebell have replied, Chohn's imagination boggled at what the answer would have been.

o o o o o o

Blessed with its customary meteorological good fortune, the Dounby Show presented a colourful spectacle, with thousands thronging the showyard to inspect a magnificent display of West Mainland livestock. As Willie Budge had foreseen, the main topic of conversation was the "test-tube" calf which Rumtodly was exhibiting, and speculation was rife as to whether it would steal the honours from Quoydunt's champion of champions. The speculation, in fact, encouraged Mansie Foubister, grieve at Quoydunt, to open a book on the outcome, and he did considerable business, the betting slightly favouring a Rumtodly victory.

Chohn Clouston stood in Bluebell's pen, giving the great animal a last touch-up before taking him on parade. He looked more confident than he felt, for though he declared unhesitatingly to all inquiries that Bluebell would win hands down, he felt some inward doubts about this. He had not yet condescended to go and view the Rumtodly calf, but he was about the only individual in the showyard who hadn't, and the reports coming back were that it was beyond question a great calf.

Generally it is Bluebell who draws the admiring multitudes at a show, but on this occasion the noble bull was playing second fiddle as a point of interest to the test-tube calf, whose pen was surrounded by a seething mob of spectators. Chohn felt a pang at this, but consoled himself with the reflection that the calf had only novelty value. Equally large crowds, he reminded Peedie Tam, had thronged to see the pig with two tails which had been one of the exhibits at a show of the past.

Bluebell himself was, as always, supremely unconcerned by the occasion. It was all the same to him whether he was watched by thousands or by none. Glancing neither to left nor to right, he chewed a piece of turnip with the imperturbability of a French aristocrat ascending the steps of the guillotine.

At length came the summons for owners of pure-bred Aberdeen-Angus bulls to lead their exhibits to the judging ring. This was a formality as far as Bluebell was concerned, the only question being which animal would be second, but Chohn took the opportunity to study the judges keenly. They were both hard-bitten farmers from Aberdeenshire, the one a squat, shaggy veteran in hairy tweeds named Donald McShuggle, the other a considerably younger man, spruce and dapper in polished leggings, cord breeches, and green pork-pie hat, his name Mortimer Rattray. It was Rattray upon whom Chohn's eyes dwelt longest. This, he felt, was the man he had to fear, a farmer of the modern school, a man who probably called proteins and carbohydrates by their first names, and probably regarded artificial insemination as heaven's gift to cattle-breeding. At all events neither judge had any hesitation about awarding the first-prize ticket to Bluebell, and Chohn led the great bull back to his pen, told Peedie Tam to keep a watchful eye on him, and set off to weigh up the Rumtodly calf.

Elbowing his way through the mob which swarmed around the pen, he surveyed Bluebell's challenger with interest and grudging admiration. There was no gainsaying the fact that it was a grand animal, and the more he looked at it the more he wondered that the union of the needle and a very so-so black cow could have produced such an impressive result.

His eye met that of Cuthbert Harcus, and a smirk overspread the master of Rumtodly's face.

"Weel, Quoydunt," he jeered, "thoo're come tae see the new champion, er thoo?"

"The champion's no decided yet," replied Chohn evenly.

"This is the champion," stated Harcus, slapping his calf on the rump. "Hid's all ower ber the shoutin', so thoo kin cheust start winderin' whit thoo're gaun tae pit on thee mantelpiece in the pliss o' the cup."

Chohn glanced at the calf again, and back at Harcus.

"I thowt," he said deliberately, "thoo wur a fermer, Rumtodly, bit noo thoo're start breedin' freaks it wid be better tae thee tae choin a circus."

He had the satisfaction of hearing an appreciative titter from the crowd, and of seeing a dull flush mount to Harcus's face. As he moved away Harcus snarled after him. "Soor grepps, Quoydunt. Wae'll see whar laughs the loodest in a peedie while."

The judging went slowly on. Once again Bluebell entered the arena, to compete for the special prize for bulls, all varieties, and once again it was a piece of cake. Chohn added one more ticket to his large collection. Meanwhile, however, the Rumtodly calf had been mowing down all opposition in its own class, and had accumulated an impressive assortment of special awards. As the climax of the shoe approached, it was obvious, to even the most untutored eye, that as far as the championship was concerned there were only two animals in it, Bluebell and the calf, and there was scarcely a pin to choose between them.

When at length a leathern-lunged steward bawled through the loudspeaker, "The chudges will noo decide the championship o' the cattle sections," excitement was at fever heat, and the mass of people round the cattle ring exceeded the record crowd at an inter-county football match.

Bluebell, led by Chohn, was first to enter, a mighty gleaming black bulk, superb in dignity and carriage, muscles rippling under his glossy skin, and suggesting, for all his dignity, the latent power of a time bomb. Harcus of Rumtodly, a smug, complacent grin on his unhandsome face, followed with his calf, also a magnificent specimen, full of spirit and diablerie, bucking with the friskiness of youth, and tugging eagerly at its halter.

"Boy," said Esau Mainland of Drydivot to his son Tristram, "if yin's whit a needle kin dae, a'm haff in the mind o' treyin' id mesel."

"Id's a grand calf," admitted Tristram, "bit I wid pit Bluebell aheid o'd, bit the chudges will hiv a herd chob decidin'."

Messrs McShuggle and Rattray did, in fact, look as if they found their task an onerous one. For fully twenty minutes they ambled from calf to bull, and from bull to calf, prodding, gripping, patting, and surveying the two animals from all angles. Then they went into a lengthy huddle, from which they emerged to circle the exhibits broodingly for another fifteen minutes. The suspense became oppressive, and one highly-strung spectator, Emmanuel Matches, fainted and had to be carried to the refreshment tent and revived with a large slug of whisky.

Ultimately old McShuggle appeared to have made up his mind. He crossed to Bluebell, patted him decisively on the neck, and glanced at his colleague for confirmation. A sigh went round the crowd as Rattray was seen to shake his head.

McShuggle rejoined him and they went into another huddle, throughout which the older judge could be seen gesticulating frantically and pointing at Bluebell again and again with his staff.

"I doot," said Esau Mainland, "yin Rattray wants tae gie id tae the calf."

Chohn awaited the decision with an impassive face, though he was sweating freely. Rumtodly's self-control was not so good. He was fidgeting like a man with St Vitus' Dance, and pulling the hair of his ample moustache out in handfuls.

Just when it seemed that the services of an umpire would have to be sought, Rattray made up his mind. Walking with McShuggle across to Bluebell, he slapped the great bull on the rump, and signalled to the steward who held the championship ticket.

"Bluebell's won id," shouted the overwrought Willie Budge, and a thunderous cheer went up.

Cuthbert Harcus was one who did not join in the ovation. His face went livid. His jaw dropped. He did not gnash his teeth, but that was only because he had no teeth to gnash. Uttering a torrent of oaths entirely unfitted for a showyard, he hurled himself towards the judges.

"Id's a swindle," he raved. "Id's a pit-up chob. Me calf's the best. Thoo're been bribed tae gie Clouston the deceesion, thoo scoondrels."

Mortimer Rattray drew himself up in indignant wrath, but Donald McShuggle had a way, born of long experience, of dealing with obstreperous exhibitors. Drawing back a little he swung his staff, and let go a cloor that stretched the infuriated Rumtodly squirming on his back. He was still squirming when a jubilant throng carried the victorious Chohn shoulder-high from the ring.

"Yaas," said Esau Mainland reflectively to Tristram, "Bluebell is still the best. A'll peen me feth tae him yet, an' no bother aboot arteeficial insemeenation."

"Id's a swindle," raved Cuthbert Harcus. *"Id's a pit-up chob."*

The Ghost of Ezekiel Drever

Ezekiel Drever, of the croft of Foulpest, Stenwick, was a man of few words. Many are the stories told of his taciturnity. It is said, for instance, that the only words he uttered during the first five years of his married life were "I do," in answer to the parish minister's query, "Do you, Ezekiel Drever, take this woman Ammonia Scollay, to be your lawful wedded wife?"

Ezekiel was a member for twenty years of the Stenwick Mutual Improvement Society, an organisation which, in the volume of verbiage it produces, is rivalled only by Stromness Town Council and the House of Commons. In all these twenty years Ezekiel had never missed a meeting, and had invariably been found, in his corner seat, pipe in mouth, and inscrutable of face. In those twenty years he uttered only one word, "Bruck," when one of those mechanically-minded young farmers for whom he had the deepest contempt, visualised, in a paper, the day when cows would be milked by machinery. This flight of fancy had apparently been too much even for Ezekiel to receive in silence.

One night, ten years ago, Ezekiel rose from the supper table, donned his coat and cap, and walked out of the croft into the night. He never returned. For days afterwards, police, soldiers, and Home Guards carried out an exhaustive search of the district, but Ezekiel was never found. It was assumed that he had fallen over a cliff, and his body swept out to sea. His wife did not re-marry, but she found some solace for her loss in the purchase of a parrot, which proved much more loquacious, and better company, than her husband had ever been. Indeed, Mrs Drever was frequently heard to remark that she was sorry she had not bought the parrot instead of getting married in the first place.

o o o o o o o

It was Christmas Eve, a fine night, but intensely cold. The ground was iron hard with frost, and snow lay over Stenwick to a depth of several inches. More snow was not far distant, as a huge dome of black cloud, mounting towards the moon, indicated.

Rudolph Firth, of Upperblash, hurried along the snow-covered road, intent on getting to the party to which he had been invited at Quoydunt ere a fresh fall occurred. He was already late, and he was estimating, with some irritation, that he must already have missed about five rounds of home-brewed ale.

Ahead of him, stark and forbidding in the icy desolation, loomed the parish churchyard, its tall headstones black against the sky. Rudolph is not an imaginative individual—in fact there are few in the parish more stolid than he is—but for all that he quickened his already brisk pace, feeling that he would be more comfortable once this place of death was behind him. As he came within view of the cemetery gate he started a little to see, standing beside the gate-posts, a tall, lean figure in a long black coat. His stride checked for a moment, and then he went on, reflecting that yin wis a queer place for onybody tae be standin' on a cowld night like this. As he approached, the figure did not move, nor did it pay the slightest attention to his coming. Its back was to the road, and it appeared to be staring into the churchyard.

As he came abreast of it, Rudolph cleared his throat, and said, somewhat quaveringly, "Ay, boy, id's a cowld night."

There was no reply. Rudolph, a trifle piqued, and at the same time vastly relieved, hurried on, but as he did so he shot another glance towards it, and saw the side of its face. It seemed to him vaguely familiar, but he could not place it, and he went on without seeking to make a closer inspection.

He had gone about another twenty yards when he recalled where he had seen that face before. He stopped, petrified, in his tracks. His eyes widened. His hair prickled on his scalp, and an icy finger seemed to trace its way down his spine.

"My geud," he blurted, "Id wur the fiss o' Ezekiel Draever." With a tremendous effort he forced himself to look round. The tall, lean figure was still standing at the cemetery gate. To Rudolph's horror-struck eyes it seemed the very personification of Death. Movement returned to his limbs. A wild shriek left his lips. His boots, scrabbling for a footing, churned up a smother of snow, and in an instant he was bolting up the road as if hell was behind him, as indeed, he believed, there was a fair chance that it was.

o o o o o o

In the farmhouse of Quoydunt all was gaiety. The walls reflected the spirit of the season with a colourful assortment of paper decorations, holly and mistletoe, fairy lights, and Chinese lanterns, and in one corner of the kitchen stood an attractive little Christmas Tree, laden with gifts in fancy wrappings.

The twenty or so guests were in hilarious mood. Chohn Clouston, the host, in a fantastic paper hat embellished with the legend, "Gee baby, you're swell," was dispensing home brew with a magnanimous hand, to the male members of the company at least, the ladies confining themselves to the less uplifting influence of orange squash, with a dash of sherry. The hostess, Chessie Clouston, was busy in the best room, getting ready the supper, which promised to be a corker, with turkey and mince pies, dumpling and apple tart, trifles and ice-cream, sooan scones, bere bannocks, nuts and Christmas crackers.

The kitchen was an uproarious scene, as the guests joined in a game instituted by the veteran Godfrey Ritch, which, he claimed, had been popular in Westray when he was a youth, and which consisted, simply enough, of all the males chasing all the females and trying to kiss them. Into this somewhat hectic pursuit none threw themselves with more gusto than Godfrey himself. With but brief pauses to absorb home brew, the exuberant ancient, his hoary head adorned with a sailor cap, bearing the inscription "H.M.S. Popeye," was cavorting strenuously after Veronica, the lovely landgirl of Quoydunt, wheezing, panting, bounding with incredible agility over pieces of furniture, and brushing ruthlessly aside all rivals who attempted to forestall him in the hunt.

Though Veronica was the main quarry, all the females were getting their fair share of attention. Willie Budge of Snortquoy was clattering ponderously after Mrs Janet Manson the postmistress, taking good care, however, not to catch her, for Mrs Manson is no beauty. Geordie Manson, by way of returning the compliment paid to his wife, was engaged in a hue and cry after Mrs Delphine Budge. Tristram Mainland had collared a not too reluctant Jeanick Budge in a corner, and was slerping her noisily. Timothy Cursiter, the policeman, was crawling under the sofa after Bella Budge, who had taken refuge there, and Peedie Tam was trying to drag Audrey Craigie out from behind the girnel. All, in fact, was fun and jollity, and if some of the furniture suffered in the course of the horseplay, it was, after all, Christmas time, and in any case the furniture did not belong to the guests.

Chohn Clouston sat on the outskirts of the revelry, drinking home brew in company with Eustace Rosie and Enoch Craigie, watching the proceedings with an indulgent smile, though occasionally glancing anxiously at the framed picture of his great bull Bluebell, which hung above the mantelpiece, and which now and again quivered dangerously.

"Boy Chohn," said Eustace Rosie, "ould Ritch is hivvin' a time o' hid. I hopp I hiv haff his energy when a'm eighty-siven."

"Yaas," put in Enoch Craigie, who is something of a Cassandra on such occasions, "bit wett ye, he'll pey for id the morn. He'll dae himsel' ill wi' this chumpin' aboot. In fact he'll likely keek the bucket afore Hogmeenay."

"Stoop, boy, dinna say yin," protested Chohn. "My mighty, the med Godfrey wid be if he passed awey afore he got the chance tae celeebrett Hogmeenay. Luks thoo. Luks thoo. He's got Veronica."

And indeed the hardy octogenarian had trapped Veronica between the press and the chest of drawers, and was manoeuvring his face into position for a resounding slerp. The laughing landgirl struggled frantically in his arms, producing from him the irritable roar: "Dorrin, lass, be a' paece, kin thoo no, an' stop wrigglin' like an eelack."

Achieving his kiss amid loud cheers the grinning veteran smacked his lips appreciatively, and ambled over to Chohn for another glass of home brew.

"A grand perty this, boy," he declared. "A'm niver enchoyed mesel so muckle for lang."

"Hid's a mercy," said Enoch Craigie. "Thoo'll no be feelin' ferly so gret the morn likely."

"Desh thee for a weet blanket, Enoch Craigie," shouted Godfrey. He drained his glass, wiped his dripping moustache with his sleeve, and remarked, "I could ferly go for me supper noo. Is id no ready yet?"

"Weel id'll be aboot ready," said Chohn, looking at the clock, "bit I wur wantin' tae wett till Rudolph Firth got here afore wae start the supper. He's litt."

"Dorrin' tak him," grunted Godfrey, "he's always the sam'. I niver saa a Firth yet whar could be in time for onything. His fether wur the sam'. Always ahint, like a soo's tell. An' his grandfather teu. I mind wen time—"

The door burst open with a crash, and Rudolph Firth staggered into the room. He stood there wild-eyed and staring, gasping for breath.

The revelry subsided as if someone had switched it off, for Firth's appearance was such as to compel serious attention.

Chohn's glass dropped from his hand.

"My lockars, Rudolph," he cried, "whit's comed ower thee?"

Firth's staring eyes swung on him. "Gie me a drem," he croaked, "for mercy's seck gie me a drem."

Eustace Rosie silently obliged. Rudolph Firth raised the bottle to his mouth with quivering fingers, and the glass rattled against his teeth before he imbibed a generous throatful. Spluttering he sank into a chair.

"Whit on earth's the metter wi' thee, Rudolph?" demanded Mansie, the grieve. "Thoo're as white as chack, min. Thoo luk as if thoo wur seen a ghost."

"That's id," he muttered.

"That's whit?" demanded Godfrey Ritch impatiently. "Tell iss whit's happened, buddo, an' dinno sit dortin', an' heddin' iss up fae wur supper."

"Id's cheust whit Mansie is said," stated Rudolph. "A'm—a'm seen—" he glanced furtively around him and shuddered, "a'm seen a ghost."

A short silence followed this announcement. It was broken by Eustace Rosie, who inquired in a puzzled tone, "Weel, whit's funny aboot that? Thir's noathing aboot that tae mak' thee come in all o' a deulder."

Rudolph, the colour now returning to his cheeks under the influence of company and whisky, gave him an indignant glare. "Thoo wid be in a bonny deulder theesel, Eustace Rosie, if thoo hid seen a ghost."

"Oh, a ghost?" said Eustace. "Boy, I thowt at first thoo said a gott. So id's a ghost thoo're seen, is id? Weel weel." And Eustace glanced significantly around him and winked broadly.

"Whit dis thoo mean be yin wink?" demanded Rudolph. "Dis thoo no believe me?"

"Weel, I widno go as fer as tae say that," said Eustace. "No doot thoo thowt thoo saa something. Wae kin all hiv halluceenations, especially if wur hin a grain tae drink afore comin' oot."

Rudolph jumped excitedly to his feet. "Feth a'm no hivvin' yin," he shouted. "I left me hoose as sober as a chudge, an' I saa this ghost as plain as I see thee, Eustace Rosie. An' a most dreidful sight id wur teu. Id near pat me ferly aff me heid."

Eustace shrugged his shoulders.

"Weel weel, thoo're here noo, an' neun the warse, an' wae kin start the supper. Efter thoo're stappid theesel o' turkey an' pudden thoo'll forget all this dirt aboot ghosts."

But the others were not letting the subject drop so easily as that.

"A ghost," cried Veronica. "Isn't that exciting? And on Christmas Eve too. Tell us all about it, Mr Firth."

"I dinno believe in ghosts mesel," remarked Timothy Cursiter, "bit I wid like tae hear whit id wur that frightened Rudolph. A'm niver seen onybody in the stit he wur in when he cam' in the hoose. He wur frightened oot o' his wits."

"Desh, I wurno as frightened as all that," said Rudolph, a trifle nettled. Now that the terrifying apparition had receded to a comfortable distance, he was beginning to regret his display of panic.

"Ay wur thoo," said Willie Budge firmly, "bit a'll no bleem thee for id if thoo saa a ghost. Whar's ghost wur id that thoo saa?"

"Ezekiel Draever's," said Rudolph, and his face paled again at the recollection.

There was a gasp. All but the youngest of the company remembered the tragedy of ten years ago.

"Ezekiel Draever," said Chohn Clouston huskily. "Boy, boy."

"I mind him fine," said Godfrey Ritch. "A moothless clurt, if iver thir wis wen, bit no a bed sowl. Whit's he wantin', comin' back tae haant Stenwick?"

"Whar did thoo see him?" asked Peedie Tam.

"At the getts o' the cemetery," said Firth. Fortifying himself with another draught from Eustace Rosie's bottle— Eustace looking on somewhat ruefully—he told his tale from the beginning. He told it well, so well that not a few of his listeners felt their flesh creep. Mrs Manson clutched her husband tightly by the arm, Jeanick Budge's hand stole into that of Peedie Tam, and when Chessie Clouston entered suddenly from the other room to see what was going on Mrs Budge leaped up with a wordless shriek and flung her arms round Enoch Craigie's neck.

"—An' then," concluded Rudolph, "The poo'er cam back tae me legs, an' I ran for Quoydunt for all I wur fit."

"The supper's ready noo," said Chessie Clouston.

No-one took any notice, except Mansie, who mumbled, "A'm no feelin' like me supper yet."

"Are thoo sheur id wur Ezekiel, boy?" inquired Chohn Clouston.

"As sheur as a'm stendin' here," asserted Rudolph. "Id wur the sam' long, lanky shipp. I cheust saa him fae the back, thoo kens, an' a peedie bit fae the side, bit id wur Ezekiel Draever all right. He lukked like a deid man whar hid niver been beeried."

"Weel, right enough, he niver wur beeried," pointed out old Ritch. "His body wur niver gotten."

Mansie shivered. "The fire's gaun doon," he said. "Pit on anither paet, Bella."

"I winder whit Ezekiel's ghost wur daein' geppin' in at

the cemetery?" mused Godfrey. It never entered the Mucklegutter veteran's head to doubt that it was a spectre that Rudolph Firth had seen. A firm believer in phantoms, werewolves, witches, vampires, zombies, and such-like phenomena, old Ritch claims to have been in close contact with the supernatural on numerous occasions in the course of his long and lively lifetime. "Likely winderin' whit wey he hid niver been beeried, no doot," he added.

"Stop id, boy," cried Mrs Manson, "thoo're gien' me the creeps."

"Er thoo no comin' ben for thee supper?" asked Mrs Clouston plaintively, but she was once again ignored.

"Did Ezekiel spick tae thee, Rudolph?" asked Godfrey.

"Niver oppened ids mooth or took the slightest notteece o' me," declared Rudolph.

Godfrey nodded as if this did not surprise him. "Ezekiel wur niver whit thoo wid call a yap, an' likely he will say less than iver fae he turned intae a ghost. Wur he lukkin' weel?"

"No gret."

Godfrey nodded again. This did not surprise him either, for he had never seen a particularly robust-looking ghost.

"Weel, I dinno believe in ghosts," declared Eustace Rosie loudly. "Niver did. Id's me opeenion that Rudolph wur frightened be a shedda. No sensible body believes in ghosts."

"Stoop, thoo yap o' dirt," snapped Godfrey derisively. "Thoo're bletherin' aboot whit thoo ken noathing aboot. Geud goad, I wish I hid a pound nott for every ghost a'm seen."

"If thoo think I saa a shedda, Eustace Rosie," shouted Rudolph, "whit aboot gaun an' seein' for theesel."

"Yin's an idea noo," put in Willie Budge. "I suggest that some o' iss goes tae the cemeetry an' see if thir's onybody—or onything—there. That's the only wey tae clear id up, if id wur a ghost whit Rudolph saa or no. Noo, whar'll go?"

There ensued a profound silence, during which everybody avoided everybody else's eyes.

"Noo's thee chance, Rosie," sneered Rudolph Firth, "bit maybe thoo're no ferly so brave noo."

Eustace shuffled his feet uncomfortably.

"Desh," he said, "I wid go teu, bit id's fairfil cowld ootside, an' id's start snawin' again."

"Thee feet's cowld, onywey," commented old Ritch.

"Not they," retorted Eustace, stung to the quick. "All right, a'll go, an' feenty ghost a'll see. Whar'll come wi' me?"

"Id's the wens whar says they dinno believe in ghosts whar shid go," pointed out Enoch Craigie. "Whit aboot thee, Timothy?"

Timothy Cursiter inwardly cursed himself for having been so rash as to cast doubts upon the existence of ghosts.

"A'm wantin' me supper," he hedged.

"Thoo wurno in a hurry for id a meenit ago, when Chessie cam' in tae say id wur ready," Willie Budge reminded him.

The constable met the eyes of his fiancee, Audrey Craigie, and the girl cried: "Go on, boy, show them thoo're no faird."

"Oh weel weel," said Timothy heavily.

"Whar else?" challenged Eustace. "Mansie. Whit aboot thee?"

"A'm no gaun," said Mansie instantly, paling at the mere thought. He had vivid recollections of an unpleasant experience which he had had some Christmasses ago at the haunted croft of Clapshothill, and though it had turned out to have no supernatural cause, the ordeal had left its marks upon his soul.

"A'll go," said Tristram Mainland, conscious that Veronica was watching him in speculation.

"Me hussband'll go teu," spoke up Mrs Janet Manson boldly.

"Me?" wailed Geordie, "a'm no—"

His spouse nudged him sharply.

"Thoo'll go when thoo're telt. Fock's no gaun tae say thoo're faird."

Geordie inclined his head in glum acquiescence.

"Fower will be plenty," said Chohn Clouston. "Noo, the queeker thoo git start the better, an' thee supper will be wettin' when thoo come back."

"If thoo come back," added Rudolph Firth maliciously.

Followed by a chorus of acclamation and good wishes the four ghost-hunters marched gallantly out into the snow.

o o o o o o o

The snow drifted down slowly in big, soft flakes, which clung to the coats of the four as they trudged dourly through it, their footsteps almost soundless in the thick white carpet. Each was busy with his own thoughts, and these thoughts were not particularly cheerful. Eustace Rosie was reflecting that it was one thing to profess disbelief in the supernatural in a warm, brightly-lit kitchen, surrounded by friendly faces, and quite another to hold the same conviction in this lonely, eerily silent landscape. Timothy Cursiter was wondering irritably why he had been so positive that there were no such things as ghosts; he had never seen one but that was no proof; he had never seen the North Pole either. Geordie Manson was wishing his wife had kept her big mouth shut and not landed him in this rash escapade. Even Tristram Mainland, who had set out in a carefree mood, was beginning to have some qualms about the expedition. A commando in the war, Tristram fears nothing on earth, but apparitions not of the earth were a little outside his experience.

More to take his mind off their purpose than because he felt high-spirited, Tristram presently bent down, moulded a snowball, and tossed it at Geordie Manson, hitting him in the back of the neck.

"Whit aboot a peedie snowball fight?" he suggested, but the idea, not surprisingly, fell flat.

"Stoop," snarled Geordie, while the other two favoured Tristram with glances of cold disapproval.

"Oh weel weel," said Tristram. He peered ahead through the falling snow, and added, "I kin see noathing, bit wae kinno be fer fae the cemeetry noo."

"Wae kinno be fer indeed," muttered Eustace, and his step perceptibly slowed

Timothy cleared his throat. "Id seems tae me," he began,

"that nobody in his right senses wid be stendin' aboot the cemeetry in this."

"An' even if they wur," added Eustace, "wae wid niver see them."

"So," proceeded Timothy, "id's cheust a wist o' time iss bein' oot, an' id wid be cheust as weel tae iss tae go back tae Quoydunt."

"That," said Eustace, "is cheust whit wur in me mind."

"Whariver's mind id wur in id wur a geud idea," said Geordie Manson, eagerly. "Come on, wae'll go back."

"Wett," demurred Tristram, "we'll luk aafil geups if wae go back an' say wae wur niver at the cemeetry."

"That's true teu," said Timothy, visualising the contempt he would encounter in Audrey's eyes if he returned and admitted he had not been to the cemetery.

There was an awkward silence.

"Of coorse," said Eustace, slowly, "thir's noathing tae hinder iss tae say wae are been tae the cemeetry, an' saa noathing."

Timothy brightened. So did Geordie. But Tristram threw a spanner in the works.

"No no," he announced, "a'm no gaun back tae be a leyar aboot id. Thoo kin all go back if thoo want, bit a'm gaun on tae the cemeetry."

He received three glares of concentrated dislike.

"An' when thoo're been tae the cemeetry, an' seen desh the thing, whit geud will id hiv deun thee?" demanded Eustace.

"Hid'll keep me conscience clear onywey," said Tristram doggedly.

Eustace, Timothy, and Geordie looked at one another glumly. It would be a trifle humiliating if they went back and said they had left Tristram to go on to the cemetery alone. Finally Timothy shrugged his shoulders.

"Weel weel, boy," he declared, "if thoo're gaun tae be a geup we'll all be geups, an' hed on tae the cemeetry. We'll sheur tae see noathing, for even a ghost widno be oot in this weather."

"Ghosts disno care whit like the weather is," said Tristram.

They went on, and some ten minutes elapsed.

"Desh this," said Timothy peevishly, "wae min sheurly be near the cemeetry noo."

There was a howl from Tristram, who was a few yards ahead. "Wur here," he grunted, "a'm bumped me nose on the dyke."

Eustace Rosie heaved a sigh of relief. "Weel, here wae er," he said, "An' thir's noathing tae be seen. Wae kin go back noo."

"Wae'll cheust go as far as the gett," said Tristram.

Just then the snow ceased, and the sombre outline of the cemetery wall, and the tops of tombstones, were revealed in the moonlight. Breathing hard, the four adventurers edged along till they came to the gate.

"Noathing there," said Eustace triumphantly, pointing. "Cheust whit I thowt. Id wur all a halluceenation on Rudolph Firth's pairt. Come on awey."

"I think wae shid luk inside a peep," said Tristram, "cheust tae mak' sheur."

"A'm sheur noo," said Geordie.

"An' me," declared Eustace. "Wur deun whit wae said. A'm for back."

"Er thoo faird?" asked Tristram sardonically. "I thowt thoo dinno believe on ghosts."

"Desh thee impeedence, Tristram Mainland," snorted Eustace. "A'm no faird, an' I dinno believe on ghosts. A'll go in. Lead the wey."

Tristram marched boldly in at the gate, and the others followed with a noticeable lack of enthusiasm.

"Boy," said Timothy, surveying the silent graveyard, and the tall stones that threw black pools of shadow on the white snow, "thir's no muckle stirrin' here."

"No muckle, indeed," agreed Eustace. His confidence returning, he walked forward down between several of the graves, stating: "Me grandfether wur beeried some piece aboot here. Id's herd tae pick oot the right pliss wi' all this snaw though." He bent in the shadow of a high headstone, and scraped in the snow. "Thir shid be a bress plitt—" Aware that someone was standing behind him he said, "Is that thee, Timothy?"

There was no reply. "Boy," he said, "kin thoo no—" He turned slowly and raised his head, and saw that the figure behind him was not Timothy Cursiter.

Tristram, Geordie and Timothy, standing talking to one another just inside the gate, were paralysed to hear a frightful shriek. They swung round to see Eustace Rosie bounding towards them, flapping his arms, wailing like a banshee, and gibbering. "The gh—gh—gh—" Behind him, tall and motionless, half-hidden by a headstone, was another figure.

Panic swept over them. They bolted out through the gate, and Geordie Manson, in his unreasoning terror, slammed it shut behind him in the face of the hapless Eustace. Not that this halted Eustace. He went over the closed gate like a bird in flight, and though his colleagues had a useful start on him, and were by no means loitering, he had quickly out-distanced them by about fifty yards.

Geordie Manson, finding himself last, spurted with a howl of dismay, and passed Timothy Cursiter. Timothy promptly accelerated and left Tristram in the rear. Tristram set his teeth, and caught up Geordie. And so it went on.

o o o o o o

"Is there no sign o' them comin' back yet?" asked Janet Manson anxiously.

"No yet," said Willie Budge, who was looking out of the back door.

"I hopp thir all right," said the postmistress. Her conscience was beginning to prick her for having forced her husband into the adventure. She had only a vague idea of what ghosts could do to people, but she had a shrewd suspicion that they were not things to be trifled with.

"I hopp thir all right teu," muttered Audrey Craigie, who was pacing nervously to and fro, wondering how she could have been such a fool as to have egged Timothy on to take part in this search for a ghost. If anything happened to him he would probably come back as a ghost himself, and haunt her for the rest of her life, and she would thoroughly deserve it.

"Dinno worry, lasses," said Chohn, "they'll be ower weel. They'll be back in a peedie blink, wi' a herty appeetite efter thir wack."

"Weel, I wish they wid hurry," snapped Chessie tartly, "or the supper will be ferly spoiled. Id wur a piece o' deshed nonsense them gaun awey like this, afore the supper. They dinno deserve tae get ony."

There was an exclamation from Willie, who had gone to the door again.

"Here they come, an' my mighty thir stoorin' along at some ritt. Eustace is in the front, teu. Geud I niver thowt id wur in him tae shift like yin."

A thin smile curved Rudolph Firth's lips. "Thir sheurly seen the ghost."

Willie Budge stood aside as Eustace, travelling like a jet-propelled snow-plough, flashed past the byre and outhouses, and hurled himself into the lobby of the farmhouse. Brushing Rudolph Firth and Mansie out of his way, he dived behind the girnel, and from there bawled hoarsely, "Keep id awey fae me. Keep id awey."

"Keep whit awey?" asked Peedie Tam. "Thir's noathing after thee whit I kin see."

Tristram, Timothy and Geordie had also reached the farmhouse by this time, and they came dashing into the kitchen, pell-mell, in the order mentioned, and stood panting, casting terrified glances out of the window. Reassured that nothing was pursuing them, their agitation gradually diminished, and they relaxed into chairs, and disposed of several glasses of home brew.

"Thoo kin come oot fae ahint yin girnel noo, Eustace Rosie," said old Ritch. "Thoo're seff here. Thoo eveedently saa the ghost, did thoo?"

Eustace's white face slowly appeared above the girnel, and after a long look round to satisfy himself that everyone present was a normal, flesh and blood being, he clambered out into full view.

"Y-y-yaas, I saa id," he gasped. "An' id wur the most aafil experience a'm iver hin."

"Are thoo sheur id wurno a halluceenation?" sneered Rudolph Firth.

"Id wur no halluceenation," declared Eustace emphatically. "Boy, Rudolph, thoo wur ferly right. Niver again will I say thir's no ghosts."

"What was it like, Tristram?" asked Veronica. "Was it very terrible?"

Tristram shifted a little uncomfortably.

"Weel, tae tell thee the truth, I niver got a right luk at id. Wae saa Eustace chumpin' oot fae ahint a heidstone, screakin' like a med thing, an' thir wis a shipp at the back o' him, bit wae didno wett for a right luk."

All eyes turned on Eustace, who expanded visibly.

"Tell iss whit id wur like, boy," invited Mansie deferentially.

"Id wur fairful," stated Eustace. "I wur bendin' doon, thoo sees, lukkin' for me grandfether's grave, an' this—this thing cam' right aside me, an' I turned an' lukked right in id's fiss. Id wurno as fer awey fae me as Mrs Manson is noo."

The postmistress drew away from him with a slight yelp.

"An' wur id Ezekiel Draever?" asked Godfrey Ritch.

"If I shid niver go fae here, id wur Ezekiel Draever. I saa him plain."

"An'. whit wur he like?" asked Chohn Clouston.

Eustace thought for a moment. In actual fact he had had but the barest glimpse of the apparition before taking flight, but he saw no reason to spoil a good story for lack of embellishment.

"I hopp," he said, sinking his voice, "I niver see the like o'd again. Id wore a lang black cott, right up tae the neck, an' a kep on ids heid, but the fiss—"

"Yaas," gasped Mansie, "go on."

"The fiss wurno a fiss at all. Id wur a skull."

A shudder ran through the listeners, except Rudolph Firth, who regarded Eustace with a puzzled frown. This, Rudolph felt, did not quite accord with what he had seen of the ghost.

"It's a wonder you recognised it as Ezekiel Drever at all in that case," remarked Veronica.

"Weel," replied Eustace, looking slightly confused, "id wurno ferly a skull, if thoo see whit I mean. Thir wis cheust enough o' the fiss there—no muckle, bit cheust enough, tae shaw me that id wur Ezekiel."

Chessie Clouston, who had been listening with mounting annoyance, now burst out.

"Ghost or no ghost, if thoo dinno all come an' get thee supper id'll no be worth tae tak'. Id's cheust seekenin', this deley."

"Weel weel, lass," said her husband, "we'll come noo, an' Eustace kin tell iss the rest o' his experiences at the teeble."

They all went into the best room, and sat down at the festive board. Chessie, still muttering peevishly, began to serve the long-delayed supper, and the guests tucked in with a will, while Eustace held forth about his encounter with the ghost. Its eyes, he said, had been black, empty sockets, and he had heard the rattling of its bones inside its coat.

Timothy Cursiter shifted restively. Eustace, it seemed to him, was hogging the limelight a little too much.

"I didno think id wur so dreidfil," he broke in.

Eustace laid down his knife and fork and stared at him contemptuously.

"Thoo wur a piece awey," he said. "I wur the only wen whar wur closs tae id, an' got a right luk."

"Thoo didno git a long luk, anywey," grunted Timothy, "for thee feet herdly touched the grund till thoo wur oot o' the cemeetry."

"I didno notteece thee hingan back muckle," retorted Eustace.

"Desh," said Godfrey Ritch, "a'm sorry I didno go teu. I wid hiv liked tae seen Ezekiel again, even if id wur cheust his ghost. Did he spick tae thee?"

"No a word," affirmed Eustace.

"Likely thoo didno gie him time tae spick," commented Godfrey. "Weel weel, id disno metter."

Suddenly Mrs Budge, who was nearest the door, sat up and looked round the table in puzzlement.

"Are wae all here?" she asked.

"Of corse wur all here," answered her husband. "Whit wey?"

"I thowt I hard somebody in the kitchen," said Mrs Budge slowly.

Silence fell over the table. Timothy Cursiter, stretching for another helping of dumpling, remained with his hand poised in mid-air. In the stillness there came from the next room the unmistakable sound of slow, dragging footsteps.

Eustace Rosie opened his mouth as if to speak, but no sound passed his lips. From the throat of Mansie came a small noise, like a death rattle.

"G-go and see who it is, Tristram," whispered Veronica.

Tristram did not move. Nobody moved. They sat wide-eyed, staring at the door which separated them from the kitchen. The dragging footsteps could be heard approaching the door. They reached it and stopped. The door handle turned, and the door slowly opened. In the doorway appeared a long, lean, cadaverous form.

Eustace Rosie leapt to his feet. "Id's the ghost," he screamed, and fell forward across the table in a dead faint, burying his face on the dumpling.

The scene that followed almost beggars description. The two Budge sisters, their mother, Veronica, and Audrey Craigie screamed simultaneously and fainted. Mansie sat spellbound for one instant, them went through the window at his back as if there were no window there. Peedie Tam and Tristram hurled themselves behind the piano amid a jangle of chords. Timothy Cursiter flung himself at the fireplace, and heedless of the peats that were glowing there, went up the chimney like a panic-stricken Santa Claus. Rudolph Firth, Willie Budge, Enoch Craigie and Geordie Manson followed Mansie through the shattered window. Janet Manson back-somersaulted off her chair, crashed to the floor, and squirmed under the sideboard like a scalded cobra. Chohn Clouston shoved his wife under the table, snatched up his chair, and retreated to the wall, prepared to defend his hearth and home against all the powers of darkness.

Old Godfrey Ritch sat where he was, and beckoned genially to the figure in the doorway, which had been watching the evacuation of the room with mild surprise.

"Come awey in, Ezekiel," he cried. "Whit like is id tae be a ghost?"

The apparition started, and stared at him.

"A'm no a ghost," it said, and as if in proof of this it

"Whar er thoo been all this time?" demanded Mrs Drever.

took off its cap, advanced to the table, sat down in the place lately occupied by Willie Budge, and began to dispose of turkey, stuffing, and clapshot with the voracity of a starving python.

Godfrey viewed this unspectral behaviour with some vexation.

"Lockars," he said, "I doot thoo're no a ghost right enough, Ezekiel. That's a peety noo. Weel I suppose id's no a peety in a wey, ither. Bit whar er thoo been all this 'ears? Wae thowt thoo wur deid."

Eustace Rosie stirred, extricated his face from the dumpling, looked glassily down the table, saw what he took to be the phantom making a hearty meal and promptly fainted again.

Chohn Clouston laid down his chair, passed a hand dazedly over his forehead, and gasped: "Ezekiel Draever, livin'—id kinno be. Is id thee Ezekiel?"

Ezekiel stopped chewing long enough to look up and grunt "Ay," and then he reached out, adroitly speared a roast potato with his fork, and crammed it into his mouth.

o o o o o o

Ezekiel was as laconic as ever, and it took much persistent questioning by Godfrey and Chohn to worm his story out of him. It seemed that he had indeed fallen over the cliff ten years before, and had been carried far out to sea, clinging to a piece of driftwood. He had been picked up by a ship bound for America, but with no recollection of his identity or his past history, for the shock of the experience had caused loss of memory. Reaching America he had taken a job on a farm, and done pretty well for himself, under the adopted name of Rockhill Zenith, which had struck him as sounding well, and which had an oddly familiar ring from the forgotten past. Two months ago he had received a kick from a horse, and the memory of his past life had returned to him. He had as soon as possible set sail for Orkney, giving no advance news of his coming, and had landed in Stromness off the St Ola that evening, and had walked out to his native parish. The reason why he had been prowling about the cemetery had been that, not knowing whether his wife was dead or alive, he had thought he might get information from the gravestones. He had then proceeded to Quoydunt for a bit of supper, for, being a poor sailor, he had had nothing to eat since leaving Thurso.

"Weel weel," commented Godfrey, when all had been disclosed, "id's winderfil teu. We'll no forget this Christmas Eve, for thoo're ferly terreefied all wur guests the night. Eustace Rosie said thoo wur a skeleeton, an' he hard thee bones rattlin'."

"The gappus," grunted Ezekiel.

This story would be incomplete without a mention of Ezekiel's return to his own croft. He walked in just before midnight, said "Ay" to his astounded wife, glanced broodingly at the parrot, and sat down before the fire.

"Ezekiel Draever," cried his wife when she had recovered from her astonishment, "thoo're a fine wen, wackin' in here efter all this time, cheust as if noathing hid happened. Whar er thoo been boy, for mercy's seck? Whar er thoo been?

"Oot," said Ezekiel briefly, and lit his pipe.